W9-DGP-254

Humor and the
Presidency

★ ★ ★ ★ ★ ★

Also by Gerald R. Ford

**A Time to Heal:
The Autobiography of
Gerald R. Ford**

Humor and the Presidency

****

by Gerald R. Ford

ARBOR HOUSE NEW YORK

Soc
E
176.1
F75
1987

Copyright © 1987 by The Gerald R. Ford Foundation
All rights reserved, including the right of reproduction in whole or
in part in any form. Published in the United States of America by
Arbor House Publishing Company and in Canada by Fitzhenry &
Whiteside, Ltd.

Manufactured in the United States of America

10   9   8   7   6   5   4   3   2   1

Library of Congress Cataloging in Publication Data

Ford, Gerald R. 1913–
    Humor and the Presidency.

    1. Presidents—United States—Anecdotes, facetiae,
satire, etc.   2. Ford, Gerald R., 1913–   —Humor.
3. Political satire, American.   I. Title.
E176.1.F75   1987   973.925′092′4   87-11502
ISBN: 0-87795-918-8

ROBERT MANNING
STROZIER LIBRARY

MAY 25 1988

Tallahassee, Florida

To the good and honest people who surrounded me during my time in the White House . . . my friends, my staff, and the press corps.

Contents

Humor and the Presidency

★ ★ ★ ★ ★ ★

Introduction

★ ★ ★ ★ ★ ★ ★

by Edward Bennett Williams

Gerald Ford and I have a
common denominator. We have each spent our lives in
sports, law, and politics — though not necessarily in that
order or with the same emphasis. He played football at
Michigan, coached at Yale, practiced law in Grand Rapids,
and had a slight avocational foray into politics.

Now sports, law, and politics also have a common
denominator. They are the only three occupations of man in
which one's every effort is measured by victory or defeat.
Everything you do goes into the win column or the loss
column. I call it contest living — or life in a pressure
cooker. The paradox of this lifestyle is that your greatest
performances can sometimes end up in the loss column.
Hence, the necessity for a sense of humor. It's indispensable
to survival — which accounts for the fact that no three
institutions in America have been a more prolific source of
fun and laughter than sports, law, and politics. Let's look at
how closely they are interwoven.

In my almost half-century in Washington, I've
learned a lot about the presidency, the Congress, and the
bureaucracy. As Yogi Berra, one of our great contemporary
philosophers, once remarked: "You can observe a lot just by
watching."

One of the things that I have observed by watching is
that the person who made the biggest impact on our
government during the last fifty years was a man named

3

Henry J. Bonura. Bonura was not a political scientist, an economist, a pundit, a writer, or a politician. He was a sort of drug-store philosopher who conceived what I like to call the Bonura Theory of Chance. Best known as Zeke Bonura, he played first base for the old Washington Senators in the New Deal years. Now Zeke was the worst-fielding first baseman in baseball. But every year he ended up with the best fielding average in the major leagues.

Introduction

How did he do it? He was no intellectual giant, but he understood one rule in baseball better than anyone before or since: *You can't be charged with an error unless you touch the ball.* And so Zeke Bonura assiduously avoided touching anything that looked difficult.

This has since become a guiding principle for all Washington bureaucrats. Every bureaucrat in Washington learned Zeke's lesson, and passed it on, generation to generation, administration to administration, ever since. At the age of seventy-seven, Zeke has the satisfaction of knowing that he has had the greatest impact on the Washington bureaucracy of any living American.

Another of life's truths that I have learned from observation is that when the president gets into trouble it's generally because of one of his most trusted senior aides. Let's go back thirty years to General Eisenhower. Eisenhower's principal assistant was Sherman Adams. Sherman was a great chief of staff, but he liked presents, and he used to take them from a New England industrialist named Bernard Goldfine — vicuna coats, oriental rugs, and other, more fungible gifts. Now, in return, Bernard felt that this meant he didn't have to do little ordinary things like file tax returns, respond to subpoenas from the Federal Trade Commission, or make filings with the Securities and Exchange Commission. It was all sort of a failure of communications between Bernard and Sherman.

One day back then I received a phone call from

Samuel Sears, a very fine trial lawyer in Boston, now deceased. He asked me if I would come up to Boston and defend a man who was indicted for income tax evasion. The man's name was Bernard Goldfine.

"Well, Sam," I said, "why don't you send me down the file?"

"I'm afraid there isn't much of a file," Sears replied.

"How come there isn't much of a file?"

"Well, he didn't make a return."

"I see," I said. "That's going to make it a little more difficult."

In the end, I figured I might as well meet Goldfine, so I asked Sears to bring him down to Washington.

"I can't bring him down," Sears said, "because he's doing ninety days in Danbury."

"Why is he doing ninety days in Danbury?" I asked.

"Judge Wyzansky gave him ninety days for not turning over what records he had."

"Well," I said, "I guess we'll have to meet up there."

And so we did. On an appointed day, I met Bernard Goldfine at the federal prison in Danbury, Connecticut. The warden was very gracious. He gave us the use of his office to hold the meeting.

Now Goldfine had many, many lawyers. The most unforgettable one was a fellow named Ralph Slobodkin. Ralph was a gopher. He would go for cigarettes, he would go for coffee, he would go for sandwiches. He drove Goldfine's car, and he also handled small claims for Goldfine's mills. In any case, after exchanging the basic social amenities, I said to Mr. Goldfine: "I'd like to get right to the jugular issue and not waste time. I'm sorry to tell you that I've looked over your case and you don't have any defense."

Goldfine greeted that news with stony silence. A few moments later, after I excused myself to go to the men's room, he turned to Sears and said, "Who does that young

5

smart-ass from Washington think he is, telling me I have no defense? If I had a defense, I'd have Ralph Slobodkin try the case."

Thus was born a verity that has encapsulated the rest of my life.

Introduction

Years later, I hired Vince Lombardi to coach the Washington Redskins. The first thing Lombardi did when he came into town was to ask for the films of all the games of the prior year. Then he sat down in a darkened room and began looking at the games. He'd look at them all day long. It took him thirteen or fourteen hours to see one game, because he would run every play ten or eleven times. After doing that for thirty days, he called me on the phone and said he wanted to come over and see me. So he came over, and we sat down for a drink, and he said: "I have some bad news for you. You don't have any defense."

Well, trial law prepares you for everything. "Vince," I said, "if I had a defense, I'd have Ralph Slobodkin coaching the team."

Now, in the evolution of the presidency, the Bonura Theory of Chance has slowly but inexorably showed itself. Particularly in the last century, a few occupants of the Oval Office have made imprudent, controversial observations that have subsequently caused them some embarrassment. For example . . .

Speaking at Columbia University in 1889, Grover Cleveland said: "Sensible and responsible women will never want to vote."

Speaking at the Patent Office in 1900, William McKinley said: "Everything that can possibly be invented has already been invented."

Speaking to reporters at the opening ball game at Griffith Stadium in Washington in 1924, Calvin Coolidge said: "Babe Ruth made a big mistake when he gave up pitching."

Cal quickly realized that he should stay away from controversial and potentially embarrassing subjects. And so thereafter he stayed silent. It wasn't until 1928, shortly before he left office, that he broke his silence — to proclaim: "When more and more people are thrown out of work, unemployment results."

This was regarded by Herbert Hoover as such a profound economic aphorism that in 1931 he plagiarized it.

Ever since, presidents have known that when in trouble nothing is generally the very best thing to do and always the most clever thing to say.

This principle was enshrined in international relations at Potsdam in July 1945, when Uncle Joe Stalin told President Harry Truman and Prime Minister Clement Atlee a famous old Russian parable about a man walking on the road from Minsk to Pinsk in the dead of winter. The man was plodding along when suddenly he saw a little bird on the side of the road, almost frozen to death. He picked up the little bird and nestled it into his greatcoat. Then he cradled it in his cupped hands and he breathed his warm breath on it. Before long, he felt the bird begin to pulsate as its circulation was restored and its warmth returned.

Looking for a place in which to put the bird, so that the warmth he had engendered would not be lost, he spied on the side of the road a pile of fresh manure. And he took the little bird and he put it right into the middle of the manure. Well, that did the job. The manure sustained the warmth in the little bird's body. In fact, pretty soon the bird began to feel so good that it began to chirp. It chirped happily and it chirped loudly — so loudly that it attracted the attention of a wolf lurking off in the woods. The wolf slunk down the path, padded over to the manure, reached in, took out the bird and ate it.

As Stalin told it, the Russians derive a three-fold moral from this story. First: just because somebody puts you in it, that doesn't necessarily mean he's your enemy. Second: just because somebody takes you out of it, that doesn't necessarily mean he's your friend. Third, and most important: when you're sitting in the middle of it, for the Lord's sake, keep your big mouth shut.

Perhaps with that in mind, American presidents have ever since tried to emulate Zeke Bonura, carefully avoiding the difficult chance, shunning the controversial, and eschewing all subjects of a troublesome nature. There have, of course, been a few notable lapses. For example, there was Jimmy Carter recounting his raging battles with lust, his deadly encounter with the killer rabbit, and Amy's views on nuclear proliferation. And during the 1976 presidential campaign, there was Gerald Ford proclaiming freedom for the Poles.

Out of all this have emerged some basic rules for all future presidents — the Ten Commandments of the White House.

1. The job is gargantuan. It's like mating elephants. It takes a long time to get on top of it. The whole effort is accompanied by a great deal of noise and confusion. The culmination is heralded by loud trumpeting. And then there is a two-year period of gestation before anything happens.

2. When you're up to your derriere in alligators, you have to remember that the reason you're in the job is to drain the swamp.

3. Handling the White House staff is a lot like being the manager of a baseball team. You've got to keep the five fellas who hate you from getting together with the five who are still undecided.

4. You must remember that a man with one watch is always certain what time it is. A man with two watches is never sure. The country always wants a president with one watch.

5. The first rule of the American College of Surgeons is, "Never say 'Oops!' in the operating room." The same goes for the White House. Never say "Oops!"

6. On the other hand, don't get discouraged about snafus. Try as you will to avoid the workings of Murphy's Law, it will always prevail. Remember, in 1895 there were only two cars in the entire state of Ohio, and they collided. Similarly, the chance of the bread falling to the carpet with the peanut butter-and-jelly side down increases in direct proportion to the cost of the carpet.

7. When you're at the bargaining table with the Russians, remember: a Smith & Wesson beats four aces.

8. Satchel Paige warned never to look over your shoulder because "they might be gaining on you." As president, however, you've got to look over your shoulder every once in a while — to make sure someone is following you.

9. In the fight between you and the special interests, the special interests will always prevail. When Conrad Hilton, the famous hotelman, appeared on the "Tonight Show" with Johnny Carson a number of years ago, Johnny said to him: "Okay, Conrad, now you have your chance. Look America in the eye and tell them what you think is life's most important truth." Conrad furrowed his brow and reflected for a moment. Then he said: "Always make sure that the shower curtain is inside the tub."

10. Finally — as for getting re-elected, remember that politics is the gentle art of getting votes from the poor and campaign contributions from the rich by promising to protect each from the other. And if you don't get re-elected, follow Zusmann's Rule for Ex-president's Symposiums: a successful symposium depends on the ratio of thinking to drinking and meeting to eating.

Introduction

Why would Gerald Ford write a book about humor and the presidency? Humor is indispensable to democracy. It is the ingredient lacking in all the dictatorships in what seems to be an increasingly authoritarian world. It is the element that permits us to laugh at ourselves and with each other, whether we be political friends or foes.

Gerald Ford came to the presidency when the nation was bitterly divided, steeped in rancor and venom. With a gentle rein, he guided it into an era of good feeling. He bound the wounds, salved the sores, and healed the nation. History will record him as a great president. I will always think of him as a great friend, a great American, and a great human being.

One

What's So Funny About the Presidency?
★ ★ ★ ★ ★ ★ ★

In 1981 we opened the Gerald
R. Ford Library and Museum to the public. It was a grand
and glorious September day that found 100,000 people
massing in Grand Rapids, including President Reagan,
Vice President Bush, former President Giscard d'Estaing of
France, President Lopez Portillo of Mexico, Prime Minister
Pierre Trudeau of Canada, Foreign Minister Sonoda of
Japan, and many others, to dedicate the newly completed
building.

Over the years since then, we have had the good
fortune to host many fine events at both the Library and
Museum. At various times, we have welcomed former
presidents, former secretaries of state, other cabinet officers, members of Congress, economists, scholars, and entertainers. The programs have been outstanding and, I believe,
helpful to many in and out of government. After a good
number of very successful events, some members of our
foundation board and I were discussing new ideas for the
next activity at the Library or Museum. Old politicians
tend to reminisce, and that's exactly what we were doing
when my aide Bob Barrett suggested that along with the
serious matters that confronted my administration, we had
more than our share of amusing incidents and much laughter.

As the discussion went on, it was amazing how
specifically we were able to recall an occasion, a joke, or a
humorous incident. Not only did we accurately remember

the funny lines in detail, but invariably we remembered the place, the people present, and how everyone reacted. It dented my ego somewhat to realize that the lighthearted moments remained in the memory with equal or greater prominence than many more substantive occasions. Like it or not, deficits rise and fall (one hopes), campaigns come and go, but a good joke goes on like "Tennyson's Brook."

Gerald R. Ford

With that as background, we decided that the subject of humor and the presidency might be worth some serious consideration. So we asked ourselves who would come to Grand Rapids to discuss humor and the presidency with Jerry Ford. Who *should* come? The list started to build. Art Buchwald, Mark Russell, Chevy Chase, Mort Sahl, Robert Klein, Pat Paulson. Could I actually consider bringing such a group of "irascible muggers" together?

These entertainers would end up doing a spectacular job providing mirth and laughter, but they were only part of the impressive group assembled. We also had to recognize the influence and effect of cartoonists: they, with their small pens and bottles of black India ink, are always poised and ready to depict graphically the latest foible or folly that we in public life seemed destined to commit. So to Grand Rapids they came: Paul Conrad, Pat Oliphant, Jeff Mac-Nelly, Mike Peters, Draper Hill, Paul Szep, and Berke Breathed.

Time, I found, had dulled my memory. I had forgotten how perceptive and tough these wits could be. I sat there and marveled at their quick and artful strokes. Each of those strokes was worth hundreds of written words. I was very happy to be in Grand Rapids watching them work — and not in the Oval Office looking at their latest representation of me in the *Washington Post*.

The final ingredient consisted of the people who provided the target for the first two groups: the politicians. They too came. There was Edward Bennett Williams, who

14

gave one of the funniest presentations I have ever heard. And it didn't stop there. We had Tip O'Neill, Don Rumsfeld, Chuck Manatt, Lyn Nofziger, Dick Cheney, Liz Carpenter, and many others.

The seeds for this gathering in Grand Rapids were sowed back in 1974, when I quite unexpectedly found myself, first, Vice President, then President of the United States of America. I had been through some difficult times with many of those who were now coming to reminisce with me about humor and the presidency, and that shared experience made itself felt in terms of warmth, candor, and humor. For the most part, despite all that we had been through, thinking back to those old days was, in this company, a pleasant chore. After two days together, we all wound up very happy and proud of what had unfolded. Quite frankly, I laughed more than I had in years.

Humor and the Presidency

★ ★ ★

There are two ways to become an authority on humor. The first way is to be one of the perpetrators. You know them: comedians, satirists, cartoonists, and impersonators. The second way to gain such credentials is to be the victim of their merciless talents. As such a victim, I take a backseat to no one as far as humor is concerned.

I clearly remember attending the 1975 Gridiron Dinner in Washington (I'll have more to say about the Gridiron Club later). After an evening of hilarious and very pointed humor, I made these remarks:

> I've learned how much of a lifesaving medicine a little laughter is for presidents. So if a fine evening of fun and friendship like this is good for presidents, it must also be good for America.

The Gridiron Club nurtures this great national asset. And I'm very glad we can all poke gentle jokes at ourselves and one another just this way — singeing without really burning — and I hope it will always stay that way.

Americans are a very diverse people, living together in many different styles and many different places. We are united more by the way we look at things than by the traditional ties of blood or belief or battles long forgotten. And when we are able to look at the brighter side of our troubles, and the lighter side of our struggles, and see the smile that lies just below the surface of our neighbor's face, I think we Americans are at our very best.

Gerald R. Ford

It wasn't always easy to believe completely in such grand remarks. Even that evening my words had been preceded by skits that included lines like: "Big Jerry's in the study hall walking up and down and chewing gum like crazy." Sitting there with a smile on your face while this sort of thing is being said isn't easy. But the truth is, you can't have humor only when you want it or how you want it.

My "unceremonious" arrival in Salzburg, Austria, in 1975, when I took a tumble down the steps of Air Force One, was another personally painful experience that reinforces the point. Falling down the stairs from Air Force One while bands are playing and troops are presenting honors is embarrassing. There was no way the press was not going to run that photo. Something like that doesn't help one's stature, but it comes with the turf when you hold public office.

Such moments were made somewhat easier because I genuinely enjoyed my association with members of the press corps. All in all, I think the profession of journalism is filled with good and bad, competent and incompetent, just like any other profession — including politics. I certainly never felt that the reporters who covered the White House were personally out to ridicule or belittle me or my presidency. Like me, they had a job to to. What's more, after the events of the previous two years — to be specific, Watergate — I was well aware that the trust between the media and the White House had been severely battered.

My association with a number of journalists, in fact, grew into friendships that I still enjoy and respect today. When I was vice president, a hard-core of news people covered me. They included Maggie Hunter of *The New York Times,* Tom DeFrank of *Newsweek,* Phil Jones of CBS, Ron Nessen of NBC, Bill Zimmerman of ABC, and, of course, Dave Kennerly of *Time* magazine. Two of this group would become very important members of my staff after I moved into 1600 Pennsylvania Avenue. Ron Nessen became my press secretary following the resignation of Jerry ter Horst, and Dave Kennerly became the official White House photographer.

David was important. Not as important as David thought he was, but he kept me and others from taking ourselves or events too seriously. I recall coming out of a meeting with Leonid Brezhnev in Vladivostok. The head of the Soviet Union and I were engaged in the most serious talks imaginable regarding arms reductions. During this particular session, Brezhnev had given me a wood representation of myself. It was a beautiful piece of work made up of many different pieces of different kinds of woods artfully arranged to create my likeness. I came out of the meeting and showed the wood "painting" to members of my staff. The idea was to make Brezhnev, who was standing at my side, feel that his gift had made the proper impression.

As I displayed it, Kennerly said, "Hey, that's great! Who is it? Frank Sinatra?"

He knew I was very displeased, but that never stopped Dave from taking a chance with a wise crack. I believe the freedom represented by such a comment was much more of an asset to me and those around me than a liability.

Gerald R. Ford

A president can very easily get isolated. To be sure, every president is insulated. Yet you must have contact with the public—with reality, if you will. Humor can be invaluable in providing such contact. Politicians, especially presidents and their immediate staffs, can take themselves too seriously. It's understandable. After all, you are dealing with the most difficult problems, and it's often hard to be terribly tolerant of those who fail to see the merits of your efforts.

At the same time, a president can forget that people and problems were there before he sat down in the Oval Office, and that people and problems will be there when he walks out of that lofty environment for the last time. With the benefit of being out of public office for more than ten years, my feeling is that humor, whether in the form of jokes, cartoons, columns, or monologues, can keep a president—or any other politician—in touch. Goodness knows we have seen enough presidents get out of touch to realize how important it is to keep that from happening.

I don't want to get too serious here and be guilty of the very sin I've just discussed. Therefore, I want to make another very important point about humor and the presidency. We had a lot of laughs in the Ford White House. To be sure, there were plenty of very difficult times, sad times, and frustrating times. The evacuation of Saigon, the *Mayaguez* incident, and the challenge of getting the economy to respond all come to mind as examples. It was my good fortune to have outstanding people on my staff and in my

Cabinet. It's also my best recollection that everyone appreciated a good laugh.

Everybody, including me, was a victim at one time or another. You must remember—on a daily basis, people like Henry Kissinger, Nelson Rockefeller, William Simon, Edward Levi, Donald Rumsfeld, and Richard Cheney might be doing battle with one another to formulate some policy or establish some position. These were not and are not shy, introverted individuals. After some very pointed and emotional discussions, it was most common to have meetings end with laughter.

The willingness to take a chance with humor is not a frivolous characteristic of an administration. The fact is, a staff member who does not fear reprisal and is not generally intimidated is going to come up with a lot more ideas and be much more creative in his or her thinking. It's bad enough to be without lighthearted moments, but it's even worse to have silence when you need a good analysis, proposal, or speech. It wouldn't surprise me if there was a measurable correlation between humor in an administration and the popularity of that administration's policies. If a president starts to put restraints on humor, the isolation and insulation to which I referred earlier will soon follow. Avoiding that state of affairs will keep a lot of people on your side during the tough times.

Humor and the Presidency

Two

Have You Heard the One About . . . ?

* * * * * * *

Why do humor and politics so often go hand in hand in the United States? Arthur Dudden, a professor of history at Bryn Mawr College and author of *The Assault of Laughter* and *Pardon Us, Mr. President,* points out that to answer this question we have to ask ourselves what is so funny about American humor.

What *is* so funny about American humor? As Dudden notes, the answer to this paramount question is not often susceptible to academic analysis, for humor has a tendency to evaporate in the heat of critical examination. It will also vanish if its subject matter, its intended thrust, is no longer timely. As the distinguished *New Yorker* writer, E. B. White, once observed, "Humor can be dissected as a frog can, but the thing dies in the process and the innards are discouraging to any but the pure scientific mind."

Divorced from all of its incentives for laughing, Dudden points out, American humor, like any other topic, abruptly becomes sober. "Example and analysis must contend in dramatic tension to sustain the context from which laughter springs," he says. "We should bear in mind that criticism of humor is a less well-developed genre than the criticism of fiction or nonfiction, drama or poetry. Criticism of humor is defined more often than not by highly personal tastes — that is, by gut reactions rather than by any widely accepted evaluative or analytical standards. What strikes one individual as hilarious can bore or disgust another."

A major obstacle to any serious appreciation of

Humor and the Presidency

American humor is that it can be barbed, disconcerting, intimidating, or even downright vicious. In 1933, Christopher Morley observed:

> There has always been something *sui generis* in the American comic spirit, though I don't know that it has ever been recognizably defined. A touch of brutality perhaps? Anger rather than humor? Various words rise to the mind — sardonic, extravagant, macabre — we reject each one, yet the mere fact that it suggests itself points to some essential hardness of spirit.

Gerald R. Ford

Dudden reminds us what Malcolm Muggeridge, one-time editor of the great British humor magazine, *Punch,* once said: that humor must occasionally be offensive or insulting to emphasize the grotesque disparity between intention and performance. "By its nature humor is anarchistic," Muggeridge wrote, "and implies, when it does not state, criticism of existing institutions, beliefs, and functionaries." Inevitably, he postulated, "All great humor is in bad taste." In Muggeridge's definition, sizable segments of American humor must be great indeed!

Mark Twain, on the other hand, celebrated humor as mankind's supreme weapon — though he believed it was employed as such too seldom. "Against the assault of laughter nothing can stand," he wrote in *The Mysterious Stranger.* Unfortunately, he added, people "are always fussing and fighting with other weapons. Do you ever use [humor]? No, you leave it lying and rusting. As a race, do you ever use it at all? No, you lack the sense and the courage."

Of course, we must have standards to apply as we examine the applications of humor to the presidency and to individual presidents themselves. Dudden offers two examples to direct us here: the humor advanced over a century ago by Artemus Ward and Henry Adams. Artemus Ward, who liked to write in the semi-literate prattle of America's small towns and rural areas, singled out George Washington as his personal favorite among all the nation's leaders — for a reason that is still convincing: Washington, Ward wrote, "never slept over." Henry Adams, the great grandson of President John Adams and the grandson of President John Quincy Adams, also thought that Washington was the nation's greatest president. He could never be equalled, Adams argued, because progress was an illusion. The direction of history, in Adams's view, was downward, not upward. The future was bound to be worse than the past. And he demonstrated this wonderfully. "A study of the presidency from Washington to Grant," he wrote, "is sufficient to disprove Darwin."

In order to appreciate how much styles of American humor have changed and evolved over the past 150 years or so, it is helpful to categorize our subject. There are various kinds of humor and various kinds of humorists, each addressing their wits and jests differently to the nation's politics. Some of the older styles are hard to find today. Some of today's styles didn't exist in the middle of the nineteenth century. But each, in varying degrees, is a very clear reflection of American democracy in action, oftentimes as public commentary on its affairs of state, and always as a testimony to the comparative freedom of utterance — in speech, press, and over the airwaves — that we enjoy in this land. As Mark Twain put it so unforgettably: "It is by the goodness of God that in our country we have these unspeakably precious things: freedom of speech, freedom of conscience, and the prudence never to practice either of them."

For the sake of convenience, Dudden divides American political humor into four categories.

First, there are what he calls the insiders. They appear early in the nineteenth century, and include figures such as Major Jack Downing, Artemus Ward, Bill Arp, Petroleum Vesuvius Nasby, and Bill Nye.

Second, there are the naysayers, or iconoclasts, who go from the end of the nineteenth century right up to today. Examples would include Ambrose Bierce, H. L. Mencken, Mort Sahl, and Philip Roth.

Gerald R. Ford

Third, there are what Dudden calls the twentieth-century court jesters, or astute observers — figures like Mr. Martin Dooley, Will Rogers, Russell Baker, Art Buchwald, Mark Russell, and Bob Orben.

Finally, there are the outsiders, the underdogs, the free spirits — humorists and satirists who operate outside the mainstream, people like Langston Hughes, "Moms" Mabley, Lenny Bruce, and Lily Tomlin.

The first of the so-called insiders to appear was a young man from Maine whose name was Sebus Smith. Starting in the 1820s, Smith wrote a series of letters to newspapers under the pseudonym of Major Jack Downing, an imaginary confidential adviser, first to a number of governors, then to a series of presidents from Andrew Jackson to Franklin Pierce. Eventually the letters were collected into a book.

Artemus Ward, who was quoted above, was famous for his imaginary interview with Abraham Lincoln. Even though he never actually met the president, his account of a mythical encounter with the great man was widely circulated and enjoyed. Lincoln himself was said to have liked it.

Like Ward, Bill Arp wrote open letters to Lincoln — though his presented the Confederacy's view of things. Needless to say, they were very popular in the South.

After the Civil War, in the contentious days of Reconstruction, another insider emerged. His real name was David Ross Lock, but he wrote under the fiery pseudonym Petroleum Vesuvius Nasby. As his pseudonym indicates, he placed himself right in the heat of the political battle that followed the war, writing a series of pieces published in 1866 under the title *Swingin' Round the Cirkle*. These aimed to help elect Democrats who would support President Andrew Johnson. Nasby's descriptions of the voters are just somewhat above the level of a hog pen. They are also very, very funny.

The insiders were followed by the naysayers, writers who opposed just about everything. Ambrose Bierce may be the first. Best known for the *Devil's Dictionary* and *Fabulous Fables,* Bierce employs a precision of language that wins a reader's admiration. For example, consider his definition of politics: "The conduct of public affairs for private advantage."

Henry L. Mencken, another naysayer who came slightly later, admired Bierce extravagantly. Mencken, too, knew how to use language. His dissection of what he called "Gamalielese" — as exemplified by President Warren Gamaliel Harding's 1921 inaugural address — remains a classic of its kind. Gamalielese, Mencken wrote, is like "a string of wet sponges," like "tattered washing hanging up on a line," like "dogs barking idiotically through endless nights," like "stale bean soup," like "college yells," and so on.

Contemporary satirists like Mort Sahl and Art Buchwald would also fit into this category.

The court jesters, as Dudden calls them, first made their appearance at the turn of the century and they continue right up through today. The first — and in many ways the greatest — of them was Finley Peter Dunne, who wrote in the guise of Mr. Martin Dooley, an Irish saloon keeper from Chicago. Reviewing Theodore Roosevelt's self-centered account of his exploits in the Spanish-American War, Mr. Dooley concludes in typically derisive fashion: "If

I was him, I would call the book *Alone in Cuba.*" Later, after TR won the 1904 election, Mr. Dooley, ever the Irish underdog, labeled the victory an "Anglo-Saxon triumph." That stung — enough so that Roosevelt sent him a letter. "Dear Laughing Philosopher, and I salute you as this," the president wrote, "I don't want to be known as for the Anglo-Saxons only, or I'll never get elected again."

Will Rogers was the first of the court jesters to move from the stage to a newspaper column to radio and motion pictures. He was truly the nation's court jester, establishing himself with such immortal lines as his observation that "we come near to having two holidays in the same week: Halloween and Election Day. And of the two, Election Day is more fun. On Halloween they put pumpkins on their heads, but on Election Day they don't have to."

The outsiders were very often from ethnic minorities: blacks like Langston Hughes and "Moms" Mabley, Jewish monologists such as Lenny Bruce. Lately, the outsiders have included a growing number of women — figures like Lily Tomlin, Joan Rivers, and Whoopi Goldberg.

In Dudden's view, the importance of the role such figures play was illustrated on July 1, 1982, when a seventeen-foot, two-ton "World's Record Apple Pie" was placed on the grounds of the Washington Monument. The plan was to slice up the huge pie and symbolically distribute the pieces to the first 3,000 people in line. Billed in news releases as a "Titanic Tart" and a "Special Tax Pie," it was designed to celebrate the start of President Reagan's ten percent tax cut.

The festivities were opened by Senator William V. Roth, one of the sponsors of the tax-cut legislation. "It's about time," Roth boomed, "for the doubters to eat humble pie." The words were barely out of his mouth when four men dressed in pillow-stuffed suits and carrying signs identifying themselves as "Reagan's Millionaire Friends"

Gerald R. Ford

pushed their way through the crowd. Before anyone could stop them, they leaped into the huge pie, stomping and squishing the filling, smashing the pastry, all the while shouting: "It's all mine! It's all mine!" Said Senator Roth, after the offenders were dragged away: "Well, obviously there *are* still a few doubters."

If there were no doubters, Dudden concludes, there would be no political humor. But doubts and doubters there always were. Political humor has always erupted as the result, and political humor there very likely always will be.

Humor and the Presidency

★ ★ ★

Presidents aren't always the victims of satirists. Occasionally we get a chance to get in a few jabs of our own. One such opportunity is the annual dinner of the Gridiron Club in Washington. James Free, the club's official historian, notes that since the Gridiron's founding in 1885, some seventeen presidents (myself included) have appeared at and participated in its programs. A requirement for such appearances is, of course, a sense of humor — the lack of which a politician admits only at his own peril. For as the essayist points out: "Men will confess to treason, arson, false teeth or a wig. How many of them will own up to a lack of a sense of humor?"

According to Mr. Free, the presidents most at home and most skilled in the Gridiron crossfire have been Franklin Roosevelt, John Kennedy, and Ronald Reagan. President Reagan, of course, developed his poise and timing as a professional actor and speaker, and he is a master at telling anecdotes to illustrate his arguments. He is also fond of — and quite expert at delivering — one-liners. "I am not worried about the deficit," he once told a Gridiron audience.

"It is big enough to take care of itself." He also once praised the Gridiron's high standard of entertainment. "It's up to the ninth grade," he said.

John Kennedy, too, had a flair for the disarming quip and the verbal counterthrust. It was a talent he demonstrated early. At the 1958 Gridiron dinner, when he was running for re-election to the Senate, he deftly undercut criticism that his father had been providing most of his campaign funds. Reaching into his pocket and pulling out what he identified to the Gridiron audience as a telegram "from my generous daddy," he read aloud the message: "Dear Jack: Don't buy a single vote more than is necessary. I'll be damned if I'm going to pay for a landslide."

Gerald R. Ford

JFK displayed similar wit at his first dinner as president. Though he welcomed constructive criticism, he told the assembled guests, he felt that those who were complaining about his decision to appoint his brother Bobby to the post of attorney general did not understand the facts. "I had a good reason for that appointment," he said. "Bobby wants to practice law and I thought he ought to get a little experience first."

Perhaps the master of the riposte was Franklin Roosevelt, who displayed a tactical skill rarely matched in political dueling. At the 1934 Gridiron dinner, H. L. Mencken heaped scorn on Roosevelt's recovery programs, claiming they had their "origins in idiocy." Speaking in response, FDR launched into what appeared to be an intemperate attack on all newspaper writers and editors. "There are managing editors in the United States . . . who never heard of Kant . . . and never read the Constitution," he declared. "And there are city editors who don't know what a symphony is or streptococcus or the statute of frauds. And there are reporters by the thousands who could not pass the entrance examinations for Harvard or Tuskegee or even Yale." As the audience squirmed uneasily,

Roosevelt then revealed that this low opinion of journalists wasn't his own. It was from the writings of the Bard of Baltimore, Henry L. Mencken.

The first president to address the Gridiron Club was Benjamin Harrison. He didn't make much of an effort to go for laughs — though his opening remark certainly went a long way towards dispelling the common perception that he was a cold fish. "This is," he told his audience of newspapermen, "the second time this week that I have been called upon to open a congress of inventors." The line has since been recycled by a number of presidents.

Humor and the Presidency

Perhaps the biggest surprise among the seventeen presidents who appeared before the club was Herbert Hoover, who was generally regarded as being somewhat thin-skinned, sober-sided, and humorless. After losing to FDR in 1932, Hoover gamely appeared at a post-election Gridiron dinner and offered an explanation of why he didn't win. After making a lengthy scientific analysis of the situation, he said, he could at last report that "as nearly as I can learn, we did not have enough votes on our side."

According to Gridiron historian Free, only one sitting president in the Gridiron's lifetime declined all invitations to club dinners — Grover Cleveland. Cleveland's attitude may be understandable, considering that his campaign for the presidency in 1884 may have been the most bitter in American history up to that time. Mr. Free says that the only evidence of humor he has found in any biography of Cleveland concerned Cleveland's 1870 campaign for district attorney of Erie County, New York. For the sake of propriety, Cleveland and his opponent agreed that each of them would drink no more than four glasses of beer a day for the duration of the campaign. A few days later, they got together and amended their pact. From then on, they agreed, a glass of beer would be defined as a full tankard.

Of course, appearances at the Gridiron club are

31

hardly the only chance presidents get to employ humor. Gerald Gardner, the author and political wit, is something of an authority on the subject. According to his research, he says, humor is a wonderful device for a president to employ — not just to get through the tensions of the day, but to persuade and to influence and to communicate. It's also a marvelous device, he notes, for dealing with issues that a president would really prefer not to confront directly. For example, Ronald Reagan has employed humor very adroitly to laugh away the issue of age, the charge that he might be too old to serve as president. (Gardner notes that President Reagan has been employing humor for this particular purpose for nearly fifty years now.)

Gerald R. Ford

You may recall that in his second debate with Walter Mondale in the 1984 campaign, President Reagan laid the age question to rest with the inspired line: "I won't make age an issue in this campaign. I will not exploit my opponent's youth and inexperience." More recently, he diffused the issue even more, pointing out: "When Andrew Jackson left the White House, he was seventy-five, and he was still vigorous. I know that because he told me."

John Kennedy was also very effective in laughing away issues, such as the question of his father's wealth or the appointment of his brother as attorney general. He was especially good at using it to dispose of the issue of religion. "The reporters are constantly asking me my views of the Pope's infallibility," he said during his 1960 campaign for the presidency. "And so I asked my friend, Cardinal Spellman, what I should say when reporters ask me whether I feel the Pope is infallible. And Cardinal Spellman said, 'I don't know what to tell you, Senator. All I know is that he keeps calling me Spillman.'"

Gardner, who travelled with Bobby Kennedy when he ran for the Senate in New York, notes that RFK shared his older brother's penchant for and adroitness with humor.

Bobby's chief vulnerability as a candidate was the charge that he was a carpetbagger. The Kennedys, of course, are associated with Boston, and Bobby was running in New York. As Gardner notes, that's a long run. Anyway, Bobby disposed of the carpetbagger issue with a line he used at the beginning of each of his speeches. "People ask me why I came to New York," he would say. "You see, I was reading in the newspaper that California had passed New York in population, so I turned to my wife and I said, 'What can we do?'"

Bobby also had to deal with the charge that he was ruthless, which he did once again by laughing it away. "You know, people call me ruthless," he would say. "I am not ruthless. And if I find the man who's been calling me that, I'll destroy him."

Self-deprecating humor is probably the most effective kind of humor for a president. But not everyone knows how to use it. Gardner notes that they used to say that Jimmy Carter's idea of self-deprecating humor was to insult his staff. Adlai Stevenson, on the other hand, had a positive gift for self-deprecating wit. For example, he used to tell of being at the Democratic convention and encountering a noticeably pregnant pro-Stevenson delegate carrying a sign that proclaimed, "Adlai's the Man!"

Public figures can also employ humor with great effect when they are faced with a hostile audience. Gardner recalls the time Governor Stevenson appeared before a Baptist convention in Houston during one of his races against Dwight Eisenhower. By way of introducing him to the crowd, the head of the convention said: "Governor Stevenson, before I introduce you, I want to make it clear that you are here as a courtesy, because Dr. Norman Vincent Peale has already instructed us to vote for your opponent. Ladies and gentlemen, Governor Stevenson." Without missing a beat, Stevenson crossed to the micro-

Without missing a beat, Stevenson crossed to the microphone and said: "Well, speaking as a Christian, I would like to say that I find the Apostle Paul appealing and the Apostle Peale appalling."

Richard Nixon did not have any of the spontaneous humor that characterized Stevenson or Kennedy. Still, there were occasions when the Nixonian wit did make an appearance. One of those occasions was related to Gardner by Ted Sorensen, who was President Kennedy's chief speechwriter. It seems that on the day following President Kennedy's famous inaugural address, Nixon approached Sorensen and said, "Ted, I have to admit that I listened to that inaugural address yesterday, and there were some words that Jack Kennedy said that I wish I had said."

"Well, thank you, Mr. Vice President," Sorensen replied. "I guess you mean the part about asking not what your country can do for you."

"No, no, no," Nixon shot back. "I mean the part about 'I do solemnly swear . . .'"

Lyndon Johnson's humor was more folksy and earthier than Kennedy's humor. Going from Kennedy to Johnson, Gardner quips, was a little like going from Noel Coward to the Dukes of Hazzard.

Johnson was a great teacher, and he used humor to instruct. For example, on one occasion LBJ was addressing a group of agency heads in the East Room of the White House and he was trying to convey to them the necessity of cutting the federal budget. To help get the message across, he told them a story about a young Texas boy who applies for a job on the railroad that runs right by his house.

"Well, young fella," the foreman tells him, "I'm going to ask you a question. You answer it right, you've got a job. Suppose you're standing at the switch. You look to the east and you see a locomotive heading west down the track at see, on the same track, a locomotive heading east at eighty miles an hour. Now what do you do?"

The boy thinks for a moment, and then he says: "I run into the house and I get my brother."

"Your brother?" the foreman yells. "Why on God's earth would you get your brother?"

"Well," says the boy, "he's never seen a train wreck."

Gardner describes my own sense of humor as "genial." And it's true, as he says, that I often make myself the butt of many of my own jokes. One of Gardner's favorites is the one I tell about the time I gave a speech in Omaha. After the speech, I went to a reception that was being held elsewhere in town. A sweet little old lady came up to me, put her gloved hand in mine, and said, "I hear you spoke here tonight."

Humor and the Presidency

"Oh, it was nothing," I replied modestly.

"Yes," the little old lady nodded, "that's what I heard."

In Gardner's view, Jimmy Carter's humor was more on the sardonic side. He used to needle his brother Billy on occasion. "I've tried to involve Billy in the government," he once said. "I was going to put the CIA and the FBI together, but Billy said he wouldn't head an agency that he couldn't spell."

Ronald Reagan, of course, uses humor very effectively to ingratiate himself with the electorate. According to Gardner, this may account for his immense popularity even among people who disapprove of his policies. Mark Russell made this point by wryly observing that Reagan was "swept back into office on a tide of disapproval."

Wherever he goes, Gardner notes, Mr. Reagan tends to put people at ease with some bit of humor that's tied to the locale. One good example of this was a story he told once in Maine. It concerned a Texan on a visit to Maine who asked a local farmer how big his spread was.

35

"Well," the New Englander answered, "it runs past that fence, then goes over the hill and down to the creek. How big is your spread in Texas?"

"Oh, my spread," the Texan boomed, "well, I can get in my car and I can drive for an hour and a half before I get to the boundary."

"Yep," the New Englander replied, "I once had a car like that."

Gerald R. Ford   President Reagan also uses humor to attack. Once recently, introducing Bob Hope at a banquet, he said: "You know, Bob Hope has two great loves. He loves to entertain the troops and he loves golf. Just the other day he asked me, 'What's your handicap?' And I said, 'Congress'."

Mr. Reagan also has used humor to attack communism. One of his favorite jokes in this vein is a story that he told Mikhail Gorbachev at their summit in Geneva. It concerned an American and a Soviet citizen who were comparing their forms of government. "In my country," the American said, "I can walk into the Oval Office in the White House, and I can slam my fist on the desk, and I can say that I don't like the way Ronald Reagan is running the United States."

"Well," the Soviet citizen replied, "I can do the same thing in the Politburo. I can go into Gorbachev's office, and slam my fist on his desk, and say that I don't like the way Ronald Reagan is running the United States."

In Gardner's view, one of the most trenchant comments on the subject of humor and the presidency was John Kennedy's observation that there are three things in life that are real: "God, human folly, and laughter." As Kennedy pointed out, "The first two are beyond our comprehension, so we'll just have to make the best of the third."

★ ★ ★

36

Another authority on humor with a particular expertise in political wit is Robert Orben. A longtime comedy writer, author of forty-six books of humor, and a former speechwriter of mine, Orben has been described as the "master of the one-liner." His comments on the subject are especially illuminating.

Why, he asks, should a president of the United States, in addition to bearing the heavy burdens of office, have to worry about going to any number of prestigious events in Washington and being funny? Why does a president, who may be working on a foreign policy address that will have an impact on the entire world, be concerned that same week about putting together eight minutes of boffo jokes for the Gridiron dinner? The answer, Orben says, is that appearing and performing at these functions is really no longer optional for a president. The chance to be seen as a warm, relaxed human being with a twinkle-in-the-eye approach to himself and politics is just too good an opportunity to be missed.

Why is humor so important? For one thing, as Orben points out, Americans, perhaps more than any other national group, are a laughing people. We enjoy laughing — especially at ourselves. That's why self-deprecating humor works so well. Perhaps more important, Orben notes, when a president gives a speech there is always a huge psychological, emotional, and physical separation between him and his audience. Here is this enormously powerful figure standing behind an impressive lectern, raised above the audience, speaking almost in the manner of a messenger of God. Psychologically and emotionally, this is the wrong attitude, the wrong relationship, for any speaker. And it's particularly wrong for a president who needs and wants the cooperation and support of his listeners.

But humor can close this gap. Humor reaches out with a warm, affectionate arm and says to the audience, "I

Humor and the Presidency

37

am one of you. I understand you." And, implicitly, it adds: "I will do something about your problems." If you can laugh together, you can hope together.

In the political arena, humor can go a step further in this bonding process. For humor is the ideal way to turn around a bad situation. When done right, it can be magic.

Orben's favorite example of this concerns the time, early in 1975, when I accepted an invitation to speak to the students and faculty of the University of Notre Dame at their Field House in South Bend, Indiana. Here is how he tells the story:

Gerald R. Ford

> Nineteen seventy-five wasn't the best year for a president of the United States to go onto a college campus. We were in a recession. Unemployment was a growing problem. And while the United States no longer had a combat role in Vietnam, student feelings about the war still ran high, and there were numerous campus demonstrations, some of them violent. In fact, just six months earlier, the presidential party had been virtually chased into the back door of a field house at the University of Vermont. I was one of the last of the party to get in before the door was closed, and I can still remember the looks of anxiety on the faces of the police and the Secret Service.
>
> So while we had been assured by one and all that we would get a friendly reception at Notre Dame, there was an overlay of concern. Since President Ford was, and is, a believer in the healing power of humor, he wanted to begin by reaching out to this audience with laughter. And so we devoted a considerable amount of time and thought to the opening remarks. Finally, from a few dozen options, the President put his money on

one joke. This is how the president opened his speech:

"As your next-door neighbor from Michigan, I have always been impressed by the outstanding record of the students of the University of Notre Dame. They have always been leaders in academic achievement and social concern and sports prowess. And now once again you are blazing new paths in the development of new concepts in mass transportation. Some communities have the monorail. Some have the subway. Notre Dame has the quickie."

Now that may not sound very funny, but when Gerald Ford said that line — "Notre Dame has the quickie" — the place exploded. The students responded with twenty-eight seconds of solid pandemonium. By way of contrast, the average big joke in show business gets perhaps five to six seconds of audience response. President Ford got twenty-eight. Kids were laughing, cheering, applauding, standing on chairs. It was genuine pandemonium.

What was that all about? In South Bend, Indiana, in 1975, the drinking age was twenty-one years or older. Across the Michigan border, twelve miles away, the drinking age was eighteen. So the big challenge for many Notre Dame students was to figure out how they could get up to Michigan each weekend for some collegiate drinking. They solved the problem by buying themselves a bus, which they called "The Quickie."

Now what was the value of a joke like "The Quickie"? When the president was going through that calculatedly long, laborious build, the students immediately thought that he was heading along a familiar path — one of those the-future-is-yours commencement-type speeches. You could see their eyes glaze over. In fact, if you listen to a tape of the speech, you can hear one of the students yell, "Bull!" (Actually, it may have been a two-syllable word.) In any case, the remark prompted a little bit of laughter from students around him, which indicated potential hostility.

Gerald R. Ford

As a result, when the president hit the audience with "The Quickie," the students were caught completely off guard. Sometime later I watched a videotape of the president doing the joke, and while the audience was going bananas, I could see one professor turn to another professor and whisper something. The second professor looked at the first with a puzzled expression and shrugged. Obviously, the first professor had asked, "What's a quickie?" and the second had replied, "I don't know." But the students knew. The president knew. And the students knew that the president knew. At that moment, they were as one.

It isn't that the audience automatically bought everything the president had to say after that, but you can bet they were an attentive and friendly group — because the president had taken the trouble to find out about them.

Now employing humor involves taking a risk. It requires a lot of guts to lay yourself out before thousands of people and the national press with a long, yawn-producing set-up that leads eventually to an unmistakable punch line. If the joke had not worked, it would have been very embarrassing.

The alternative would have been to play it

safe. You can always get an acceptable reaction from a college audience by joking about the mystery meat in the cafeteria or praising the football team. But that sort of thing won't get the audience out of their seats. President Ford went for the touchdown.

Why humor? Nowadays, the more pertinent question would be, why not?

Three

You're Gonna Love This . . .

★ ★ ★ ★ ★ ★ ★

The impact of humorous re- **Humor and the**
marks, incidents, or cartoons that poke fun at the president **Presidency**
can be much harder on his family than on himself. As I said
earlier, the line between humor and ridicule is quickly
crossed. And a politician's family will always feel those
barbs much more than the politician himself ever will.

It becomes even more difficult for all concerned when
members of one's family become targets themselves.
Whether they like it or not, they are fair game. (Actually,
the truth of the matter is that while they may be "game,"
it's not necessarily fair.) Every member of any family that
has ever occupied the White House has vivid recollections
of incidents that they thought were unfair, if not outright
mean. In a perfect world, the family of a president would be
spared the barbs of pundits, cartoonists, columnists, and
comedians. In the real world, that's not possible, let alone
likely.

I am not suggesting that living in the White House is
a normal situation. But the families are normal, or at least
try to be. Children of presidents are happy and sad. They
get good marks and bad marks in school. They go out on
dates. They get in a little trouble now and then. These
normal things become raw material for the humorists,
comedians, and cartoonists. Coverage by the media is
constant and intense. It's not likely that it will ever be
different.

Just the same, there is another side that people in the spotlight tend to forget, or at least brush aside. With the possibility of an exception or two, I doubt there is anyone who has had the privilege of living in the White House who regrets having done so. Oh, I'm sure that you will hear comments to the contrary every now and then, but if pushed to the bottom line, presidents as well as their wives and children will tell you that their time at 1600 Pennsylvania Avenue was a positive and fortunate experience.

*Gerald R.
Ford*

There is a final point I'd like to make about this aspect of humor on a president and his family. For the most part, you get used to it, and you are better off for having had the experience.

When we first moved into the White House, Betty and I were very concerned about what effect life in the spotlight would have on our children. In the end, they each chose to handle it in their own way, sometimes with style and success, other times with frustration and failure.

Mike, our eldest, and his wife Gayle chose to keep a low profile, and were very successful in doing so.

Jack took a more participatory position, and naturally had his good moments and his bad moments. But he handled them well.

Steve had more of a "happy-go-lucky" approach, which I think significantly enhanced his ability to handle many of the things he undertook later in his life.

Susan was the youngest, and our only daughter. Naturally, we probably worried more about her than any of her older brothers. Interestingly, Susan managed quite well in handling the public attention. For one thing, she had more than her share of teenage indifference. That, combined with a very strong will and her determination to have the types of experiences she felt she was entitled to as a young woman, caused her to survive the experience quite nicely.

Betty and I were very satisfied with — and, in fact, rather proud of — how well the children weathered the sometimes stormy conditions of public life in the White House. When I lost the 1976 election, we stood together as a family in the White House press room. Certainly, we'd have rather won than lost, but at least we had survived. And I think we were stronger for it all. Later, that strength would be demonstrated when Betty decided to enter the Long Beach Naval Hospital to be treated for her chemical dependency on prescribed drugs and alcohol. Our strength as a family was crucial to her success.

★ ★ ★

A president makes many decisions. He is not immune to mistakes. A good number of people, on the staff and elsewhere, thought it was a mistake to let Ron Nessen, my press secretary at the time, appear on "Saturday Night Live" with Chevy Chase, the gifted comedian who had become quite famous for his impression of me as a paragon of clumsiness.

Military men speak in terms of strategy and tactics. The first deals with long-term consequences, while the second is concerned with more immediate effects. Tactically, it was probably a mistake to have Ron on the show. The media had already shown a strong penchant for focusing on my shortcomings. For those people who wanted to see me in less than "grand and presidential" circumstances, Chevy Chase and "Saturday Night Live" provided them with plenty of grist for their mills. Strategically, however, the decision doesn't seem as wrong today as some people thought it was back in 1975. Even if we did make an error, I believe it is always better to err on the side of more exposure and access rather than less. At that time, the

47

media and the general public still resented any hint of "imperial" trappings in connection with the presidency or the White House.

Gerald R. Ford

Having said all this, I must be truthful and admit that the comic representations of me by Chevy Chase and others were sometimes hard for me and my family to take. Though it was essential to grin and bear it, it could and did hurt. If you'll forgive me some immodesty, I thought myself to be a fair athlete. During my time in the White House, I played golf with better than average success. I enjoyed tennis and had very competitive matches with Alexander Haig, George Bush, Don Rumsfeld, Dave Kennerly, Bob Barrett, and others. I skiied every winter, and could be rated as intermediate to expert. And, finally, I swam every day.

With that in mind, I would then watch Chevy Chase come crashing down a staircase as Jerry Ford. Now I ask you — was I being treated fairly?

The question is clearly rhetorical. And the answer has nothing to do with fairness. The portrayal of me as an oafish ex-jock made for good copy. It was also funny. Maybe not to me, but as much as I might have disliked it, some people were laughing. At the very least, even if no one else was going to laugh, you can be sure the Democrats would! I can just hear Tip O'Neill telephoning some journalist and saying: "This is an anonymous phone call. President Ford just tripped and fell getting up out of a chair in my office."

★ ★ ★

Some people have suggested that I handled the jokes at my expense very well, and that I thought such things "came with the turf" of being president. Let me put it this way: I developed a good exterior posture. The truth of the matter is that some of my favorite pipes have teeth marks in their stems that you wouldn't believe. This is a fact. You cannot cry out dramatically about your outrage or your indignity. That, as sure as tomorrow's sunrise, will open a floodgate that you'll never be able to close.

What kind of response can a president make, if any? Probably none by himself. Others may take up the defense of their man in the White House. (And even that can sometimes backfire, depending on who says what.) In the final analysis, you must have confidence in yourself as a human being doing the best job you can in a most difficult set of circumstances. You must also have faith in the idea that, if not in the short term, then in the long term, fairness will prevail.

It may well be true that as a result of the explosion of information made possible by the electronic coverage of the mass media, objectivity has flown out the window. I believe David Brinkley made much the same point many years ago, writing in the *Columbia Journalism Review*. At the risk of taking what he said out of context, I recall that David suggested that objectivity had become a thing of the past, and that in the years ahead journalists should instead try to seek fairness as their goal in reporting. I had, and still have, that faith in journalists. On the whole, they have been trustworthy. They have been friendly and unfriendly, but I have never felt them to be my foe.

Somewhere in this longwinded dissertation is the explanation of how I persevered in the face of humorous, satirical, or, on occasion, ridiculing assaults. All in all, I would not change too many, if any, of my experiences in life. There always were, and are today, many wonderful moments of enjoyment and laughter.

As a matter of fact, it's possible to have too much humor at times. Since I left the White House, I've had a

Humor and the Presidency

little more time for golf, and quite often my time on the links is shared with Bob Hope. Bob goes around the country commercializing on the inadequacies of my golf game. He tells people that his favorite foursome consists of Jerry Ford, a medic, and a faith-healer. He goes on to say that I'm the only golfer he's ever known who lost a ball in the ball-washer. I must admit, playing with him is sometimes a challenge to my concentration. But I love him and every one of his wisecracks about my game.

Gerald R. Ford

Bob Hope's humor is a perfect example of how to poke fun and not cross over that line into ridicule. Bob also plays no favorites from a partisan point of view. And each year, I have a chance to get back at him when he asks me to write a letter for the program of his Bob Hope Golf Classic. In 1987 the following letter appeared in the program:

Dear Bob,

It is again my honor and privilege to join you for the 1987 Bob Hope Chrysler Classic. Each year the traditions of the Classic continue to grow like your reputation for having played golf with more presidents than any other person.

For example, your fans and spectators might not know that the first president to be your friend was Ulysses Grant. He, of course, was indebted to you for having entertained the troops at Gettysburg and Shiloh. Old golfers still love to sit and listen to the wonderful stories about your golf game with William Jennings Bryan, Stonewall Jackson, and Calvin Coolidge.

Although you have taken some license in ridiculing my golf game before large audiences, I am nevertheless proud that you treat me in a manner equal to that of other presidents you have known, such as Teddy Roosevelt, James Polk, and Andy Jackson.

Finally, it must please you to have Chrysler as your major sponsor. As a five-year-old youngster, I remember that picture of you sitting in the first Chrysler ever manufactured.

All of us who love you can look ahead to the day when you will return from some galaxy having entertained the troops fighting Star Wars. Most likely, if you are true to form, you will tee it up the next morning with the President of the United States, who at this moment is somewhere in this great country having his or her diaper changed.

This letter each year gives me a small opportunity to counter some of the great jokes you tell at my expense. Have no doubt about it, dear friend, you are a tradition and you richly and generously have given this country so many things over so many years. Betty and I join with all your friends in the desert and elsewhere who wish you the most successful and exciting Classic ever.

P.S. Start hitting on Tip O'Neill. He's out of work, too!

Humor and the Presidency

By including this letter, I suppose I'm trying to make the point that humor, with its give and take, is still a part of my life today. I may have gotten to the presidency, but I still think of myself as an average American who worked hard and got his fair share of good breaks.

Four

The Cartoonists

★★★★★★★

Fairness, of course, has never been a major concern of satirists — particularly the political cartoonists, who can make reading the morning paper such a painful experience for a president. According to Paul Conrad, the Pulitzer Prize–winning cartoonist of the *Los Angeles Times,* the job of the political cartoonist is "to make two and two equal five" — to take two apparently unrelated items from the day's news and "pull them together." By way of example, he offers the following: "Two of the hottest issues these days are the Federal deficit, which now totals over $2 trillion, and President Reagan's war on drugs. Well, why not combine the two and show the president snorting a pile of cocaine that's labeled 'deficits'? You could caption it, 'Speaking of addictions . . .' "

But how far can a political cartoonist go? What constitutes fair comment and what constitutes bad taste? Conrad recalls the time he drew a cartoon commenting on a battle over water rights that was raging in California. "The cartoon showed northern California urinating on southern California," he remembers. "Of course, it was drawn from the perspective of Montana. Well, the day after it appeared in the paper, my publisher showed up and said, 'Con, brilliant cartoon, but it never should have run.' I asked him what he didn't like, and he said it was a question of taste. I said, 'Tom, it seems to me that if I had drawn that image from the point of view of Arizona — now *that* would have been bad taste."

Humor and the Presidency

Like many cartoonists, Conrad insists that he has nothing personal against the politicians he lampoons. "All we do is take the issues," he says, "and we assume that the president can take the heat or the plaudits — depending on how the issues come out."

Not everyone feels that way. Burke Breathed, the brilliant young cartoonist whose syndicated comic strip, "Bloom County," appears in over 900 newspapers, thinks a little personal animosity is probably good for the soul — at least for the cartoonist's soul. This is how he explains his view of things:

Gerald R. Ford

The political cartoonist views the president much the same way as many people view God — which is to say, if he didn't exist, we probably would have to create him. Still, as a satirist, I must admit that I am dismayed by the apparent warmth felt by President Ford toward political cartoonists. Be assured — the president's ability to pick up the daily paper, peruse one of our sketched jabs at one of his policies or personal peccadilloes, laugh heartily, show the cartoon to his staff, congratulate himself privately on his ability to appreciate humor even when it is directed against him, and then, horror of horrors, request the original to hang in his office — this ability does not please us. Or if it does, we don't admit it. For my part, the thought actually fills my heart with dread and terror.

Now, while most of us will pretend that our preferred audience for our cartoons is the mighty and seething masses of the reading public, deep inside our dark, evil, and anarchistic hearts is the quiet passion to have the exact target of our wit — often the president himself — read the damn thing himself with his morning coffee in the Oval Office. Again, few of us will admit that this is our primary concern, but I think that deep within ourselves this fantasy lives. Of course, what we fantasize is not that the president will chuckle or laugh when he reads our cartoon. No, deep inside all of us is a secret fantasy that involves the most powerful individual on the planet, the leader of the free world, ripping our cartoon out of the morning paper, stomping down the White House hallways snorting, steaming, and spitting in a tirade of wrath and vengeance, and then taping the cartoon to the toilet paper in the nearest bathroom.

This is our dream — a dream I have yet to fulfill.

No, what happens to me and to "Bloom County" is the very worst thing that can happen to a cartoonist and his cartoons. The targets of my barbs always call and ask for the original drawing.

This is failure.

Not too long ago I did a cartoon making fun of President Reagan. What happened? The White House asked me for the original, the President signed it, and then hung it prominently above his desk. That tore my heart out.

Recently, I did a piece on Barry Manilow, the pop singer, in which I questioned his masculinity. The *Washington Post* lawyer said Manilow would sue. Of course he didn't. Instead, he wrote and asked for the original — as I recall, with a card that smelled faintly of lilacs.

Perhaps it's a phenomenon of the comic page (where my strip appears), as opposed to the editorial page (where most political cartoons are placed), which makes it virtually impossible to insult anybody. And, believe me, I've done my utmost to insult people. Yet, without fail, they continue to ask for the originals. As far as I'm concerned, there's something about seeing yourself on the comic page that affects everybody the wrong way.

Gerald R. Ford

Let me tell you about the worst thing that ever happened to me — the day the chief called me himself. It was in October 1985, and I was taking a shower when word came that President Reagan was on the telephone. I rushed out, then stood there dripping wet and naked as the leader of the free world complimented me on the previous Sunday's "Bloom County," which particularly speared one of his policies. My heart sank. It seems the president had spied an image of his wife, Nancy, in the third panel. It was, he told me, a very flattering caricature of her. My heart sank again.

Then he asked for the original. I looked for my Exacto knife to slit my throat.

Today, the original strip hangs somewhere in the White House basement, complete with the flattering image of Nancy Reagan in panel number three. However, I don't lose too much sleep over that fact because secretly I know that the flattering caricature of the First Lady was not from my hand at all. It was a photocopy of a photograph of her from a 1968 campaign postcard. I can live with that.

Art Buchwald, the popular satirist, says he's never been contacted directly by a president about a column of his. But he does claim to have heard the following story from Bill Moyers, who was an aide to Lyndon Johnson before going on to become a distinguished publisher and television commentator. It seems that, during the Johnson era, Moyers was sitting at his desk in his White House office, laughing uproariously. LBJ happened to be walking by, and he stuck his head into Moyers's office to ask what he was laughing at.

"I'm reading Buchwald," Moyers gasped, the tears fairly rolling down his cheeks.

The president favored Moyers with one of those baleful glares for which he was well known. "You think he's funny?" LBJ snapped.

Moyers straightened up. "No, sir!" he replied.

Knowing whose side you are on may be the first rule of politics — and that goes for commentators as well as practitioners. Paul Szep, whose political cartoons have won him two Pulitzer Prizes, tells the story of the time he and a number of other cartoonists were invited to the White House by Ronald Reagan. Excited by the news, Szep's mother told a friend that her son had just gone to Washington.

"Does he work for the government?" the friend asked.

"Oh, no," Mrs. Szep replied. "He's a cartoonist. He works *against* the government."

Jeff MacNelly, the three-time Pulitzer Prize-winner who draws the popular comic strip "Shoe," observes that political cartoonists — and political satirists in general — often have a kind of conflict of interest between what they think is good for their country and what they know is good for their business. As citizens, he notes, they appreciate the fact that "a feeling of good humor in the White House is probably a good thing. But as a satirist and cartoonist, it's much more fun to have guys in there who take themselves seriously." MacNelly's observations are characteristically sharp-edged, funny, and worth repeating:

Gerald R. Ford

> I had a lot of fun with Jimmy Carter, although he didn't have much fun with me. I remember one time I had been invited to the White House, and President Carter said, comparing me to the anti-administration editorials that my boss at the *Richmond News-Leader* used to hammer out every morning. "You're not as bad as those editorials, but almost."
>
> As usual, I didn't have any snappy reply. A few hours later, I was in my truck driving down Interstate 95, and just as I got to Fredericksburg, it came to me. What I should have said to Carter was, "You're not as bad as Warren G. Harding, but almost."
>
> That wasn't the only time I was at the White House. President Ford once invited me to a state dinner at the White House. I think King Hussein of Jordan was there. King Hussein is usually there. He shows up in Washington about every three and a half weeks, and we have to have a dinner for him. Anyway, I was invited. Needless to say, the first thing I did was to call my mother and tell her, "Mom, guess what? I'm going to the White House!"
>
> And my mother said what every mother who has a large and somewhat sloppy son would say: "Not in those dirty shoes, you aren't."
>
> Anyway, I got there, and I was standing in the reception line waiting to be introduced to President Ford and King Hussein. Now, it happened that the week before this state dinner I had done a particularly nasty cartoon about the pres-

ident. So when I got to the head of the line, President Ford turned to Hussein and said, "King, this guy's a cartoonist and he just did a great cartoon of me last week. He did me as a gorilla hanging upside down from a tree, dropping a banana."

Hussein, of course, has some problems in his country. I mean, smoking grenades tend to roll under his desk with alarming regularity. As a result, he's a pretty security-conscious kind of guy. And while we're shaking hands, I can almost hear him thinking: one, what is this guy doing out of jail — and two, why aren't there some Secret Service men between him and me?

I might add that I really don't regard myself as much of a journalist. I proved this in Salzburg, Austria, on that famous occasion when President Ford tumbled down the airplane steps and kissed the tarmac. I was the only cartoonist in the world who was actually there at the time, and all I could think of when it happened was, "Gee, I hope he didn't hurt himself." Of course, when I got home, everybody else was having a field day with it, drawing pictures of Ford with bandages all over his head.

Me, I totally missed the boat.

It is, of course, much more fun to look at cartoons than to talk about them. The following sampler provides an indication of just how potent — and diverse — a weapon the cartoonist's acid-tipped pen can be.

The granddaddy of American political cartoonists was Thomas Nast, whose drawings for Harper's Weekly *in the mid- and late-1880s set a standard for bite, wit, and graphic excellence. Among Nast's most powerful cartoons were his attacks on the corrupt Tammany Hall political machine that dominated New York politics of the era. Nast depicted Tammany as a ravenous tiger, while its leader— the infamous "Boss" Jim Tweed—was portrayed variously as a Roman emperor, a vulture, and a character out of Dickens.*

OSE.—" What are you going to do about it?"

"WHAT ARE YOU LAUGHING AT? TO THE VICTOR BELONG THE SPOILS."

A GROUP OF VULTURES WAITING FOR THE STORM TO "BLOW OVER."—"LET US *PREY*."

"They no sooner heard the cry, than, guessing how th[e]
Thief!' too, joined in the pursuit like *Good Citizens*."—"Olive[

THIEF!"

ood, they issued forth with great promptitude; and, shouting 'Stop

SOMETHING THAT DID BLOW OVER—

Tweed had insisted that the public outcry over his machine would "blow over." It did not, and after Tammany took a drubbing in the election of 1871, Nast celebrated accordingly.

Like more than a few of his successors, Nast delighted in annoying the White House. But as this 1877 cartoon shows, unlike most of his successors, he was not above caricaturing himself as well as the president.

HARPER'S WEEKLY.

JOURNAL OF CIVILIZATION

VOL. XXI.—No. 1062.] NEW YORK, SATURDAY, MAY 5, 1877. [WITH A SUPPLEMENT.
PRICE TEN CENTS.

Entered according to Act of Congress, in the Year 1877, by Harper & Brothers, in the Office of the Librarian of Congress, at Washington.

"NAY, PATIENCE, OR WE BREAK THE SINEWS."—Shakspeare.

U. S.: "Our Artist must keep cool, and sit down, and see how it works."

It was Nast who gave us two of the most enduring symbols in our American political menagerie: the Democratic donkey (as depicted in an 1879 cartoon) . . .

STRANGER THINGS HAVE HAPPENED.

HOLD ON, AND YOU MAY WALK OVER THE SLUGGISH ANIMAL UP THERE YET.

. . . and the Republican elephant (shown here in an 1884 incarnation).

THE SACRED ELEPHANT.

THIS ANIMAL IS SURE TO WIN, IF IT IS ONLY KEPT PURE AND CLEAN, AND HAS *NOT TOO HEAVY A LOAD TO CARRY.*

Cartoonists had a field day lampooning what they seemed to regard as my penchant for accidents. The fact is, it wasn't always my fault—as this 1975 drawing by Mike Peters makes clear.

"JOHNSON, YOU KEEP YOUR EYES OUT YOU WATCH FOR OPEN MAN HOLE CO HANDLE KILLER BEES AND......"

ERS AND RUNAWAY TRAINS......PETROVITCH,
BUFFALO STAMPEDES......SMITTY, YOU

Paul Szep was a bit more unkind in this 1976 cartoon, which played on the excitement over Queen Elizabeth's upcoming Bicentennial visit to Washington and a rather disparaging remark about my powers of physical coordination.

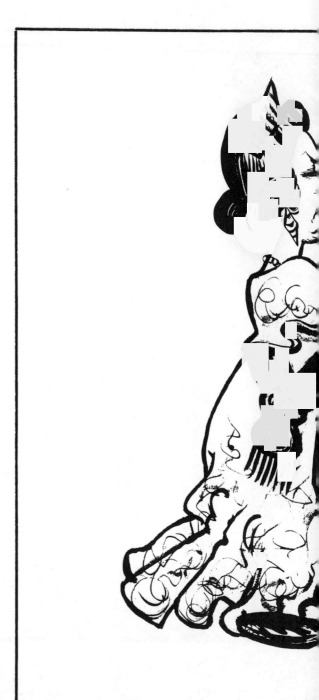

Presents, of course, are always being attacked for one decision or another. Here, in a 1976 cartoon, Pat Oliphant rakes me over the coals for pardoning former President Nixon and defending then agriculture secretary Earl Butz. (Notice the bandage Oliphant felt obliged to paste on my forehead.)

...BUT A DECENT, GOOD PERSON!

BUTZ FORGIVEN

OLIPHANT

© 1976 WASHINGTON STAR
LOS ANGELES TIMES
SYNDICATE

...AND THE
ALTERNATIVE
IS JIMMY
THE PEANUT

JERRY FORGIVEN

Some things, alas, never change. In 1971 Draper Hill traced America's involvement in Vietnam from Harry Truman to Dwight Eisenhower to John Kennedy to Lyndon Johnson. Four years later, Mike Peters extended the legacy to include Richard Nixon and me.

CONTINUITY

85

Occasionally, someone other than the president gets to take the heat. In this 1975 cartoon, Oliphant skewered Henry Kissinger for an impolitic remark he supposedly made about me. (I got the feeling, though, that Oliphant's sympathy for me was less than whole-hearted.)

'AW, C'MON, JERRY — NO

© THE LOS ANGELES
TIMES SYNDICATE
© 1975 THE WASHINGTON STAR

OLIPHANT

BANNED ISRAELI BOOK
'KISSINGER
CALLED FORD
DUMMY'

THE DUMMY KEEPS
YOU AROUND,
HANK..!

...IEVES ANYTHING I SAY, ANYWAY...'

The confusion following the 1975 Mayaguez incident prompted Oliphant to borrow from Mort Walker, the creator of the immortal cartoon GI, "Beetle Bailey." (By the way, the squinting figure with the pipe in his mouth is supposed to be defense secretary James Schlesinger, and the smiling aide with the wind-up key in his back is Oliphant's caricature of my press secretary, Ron Nessen.)

89

In this 1976 cartoon, Paul Conrad borrowed from Charles M. Schultz (of "Peanuts" fame) to remind me of a fundamental rule of politics.

LET ME HOLD THE FOOTBALL FOR YOUR CAMPAIGN KICK-OFF, MR. PRESIDENT

Copyright © 1976 Los Angeles Times. Reprinted with permission.

DELIVERANCE

WARNING
DANGEROUS
CROSSCURRENTS

Ronald Reagan gave me quite a battle for the 1976 Republican nomination. Draper Hill captured the atmosphere quite nicely in this representation of the primary campaign.

My 1976 debates with Jimmy Carter had their ups and downs. Here, Paul Szep zeros in on one of the latter. (Note the broken pipe the cartoonist has drawn under my chair. Szep and his colleagues were responsible for more than a few of those in real life.)

"I'LL BE JACK KENNE.

©THE BOSTON GLOBE

HO DO YOU WANT TO BE??"

DAYTON DAILY NEWS 1976

Mike Peters

The 1976 elections brought a new look to the White House. Here is how Mike Peters summed it up.

His enormous popularity among the voters did not earn Ronald Reagan any special treatment from the political cartoonists—as this 1984 Mike Peters drawing shows.

GREAT DEBATE #1

MacNelly Chicago Tribune.

President Reagan's economic policies were a favorite target of the cartoonists. Here, Jeff MacNelly takes aim at the president's assertion that federal budget deficits weren't as bad as some critics insisted they were.

Former White House budget director David Stockman's revelations about the origins of Reaganomics struck some critics as disingenuous. MacNelly was one of them.

Some controversial Reagan administration findings about the extent of hunger in America prompted this 1984 cartoon by Mike Peters.

105

Great Moments in Dip[lomacy]

Reagan lays a wrea[th at] the Tomb of the Unknown Advance[r]

MACNELLY Chicago Tribune.

When President Reagan visited a West German cemetery in which a number of SS troops were buried, his advancemen found themselves in trouble for not anticipating the controversy that would ensue. In typical fashion, Jeff MacNelly added some fuel to the fire.

106

Presidential appointments are always a prime target for cartoonists. In this 1985 effort, Paul Conrad takes advantage of President Reagan's show-business background to poke a little fun.

"OTHER THAN YOUR FRIENDSHIP WITH THE PRESIDENT, MR. BONZO, WHAT QUALIFIES YOU FOR THIS CABINET POSITION?"

Copyright © 1985 Los Angeles Times. Reprinted with permission.

BLOOM COUNTY

Unlike most of his colleagues, whose work generally appears on the editorial page, Berke Breathed is a denizen of the comics page. This most definitely does not mean that Breathed's popular "Bloom County" strip, which appears daily in upwards of nine hundred newspapers, isn't highly political.

by Berke Breathed

Used with permission of the Washington Post Writers Group.

BLOOM COUNTY

BY BERKE BREATHED

HARK! — I HEAR IT!

HEAR WHAT?

LISTEN... POLITICAL CHANGE IS UPON THE WIND...WHISPERING EVEN AMONG THE CONSERVATIVE DIN...

SURF MISSOURI!

NO RAIN ON THIS PARADE

6-1

IN FACT, I HEAR DIDDLY-SQUAT. WHAT ARE THEY SAYING?

"AMERICA MUST NEVER AGAIN SPILL HER BLOOD IN FUTILE WARS!!"

112

Used with permission of the Washington Post Writers Group.

BLOOM COUNTY

BY BERKE BREATHED

BINKLEY! WAKE UP! YOO HOO! TIME FOR SOME HOUSE-CLEANING!

GIANT PURPLE SNORKLEWACKER (snorklii sub-consciousii)

SHOCKED! YES, SHOCKED I AM! LOOK AT YOUR ANXIETY CLOSET! A MESS!... LITTERED WITH OLD AND AGING CONCERNS.

6-29

©1986, Washington Post Writers Group

WHAT'S THIS? ENVIRONMENTAL POLLUTION? HA!!

INDUSTRIAL WASTE DUMP IN NEAREST RIVER

SO I'M A LITTLE UNFASHIONABLE! I'LL GET HIP!... I UNDERSTAND "THE HOMELESS" ARE HOT AT THE MOMENT...

HOT SHMOT... LOOKIT THIS JUNK!.. OH... NOW LOOKIT THIS! LOOKIT THIS...

114

Used with permission of the Washington Post Writers Group.

Five

Letting Off Steam

★ ★ ★ ★ ★ ★ ★

Liz Carpenter, a longtime
and delightful fixture in Washington who served as an
executive assistant to Lyndon Johnson and as assistant
secretary of education in the Carter administration, notes
that the first president to make use of humor in a significant
way was Abraham Lincoln. In the darkest days of the Civil
War, Liz points out, Lincoln would often begin cabinet
meetings by reading the satirical stories of Artemus Ward.
This irritated some politicians, who felt the president
should be more sober and serious. One such critic, a
Congressman Arnold from New York, complained to Lincoln about the practice, asking: "How can you sit there and
read those stories knowing the casualty figures that are
coming in from Gettysburg?" Lincoln, the story goes, flung
down his book of Artemus Ward stories and turned to
Arnold, tears streaming down his face. "Mr. Arnold," he is
supposed to have said, "were it not for my little jokes, I
could not bear the burdens of this office."

Of course, as we have seen, Lincoln was hardly the
first national political leader to understand the importance
of humor. Chuck Manatt, who used to chair the Democratic
National Committee, notes that humor was used as a tool
by American politicians even before there was a United
States. Two centuries ago, at the Constitutional Convention
in Philadelphia, when Benjamin Franklin and George
Washington found themselves on opposite sides of a heated
debate over whether or not the new nation should have a

**Humor and the
Presidency**

119

standing army, they wound up turning to humor to resolve the dispute.

Not surprisingly, Washington favored having a standing army, while Franklin opposed it. As a compromise, someone proposed that the constitution allow the formation of a standing army of no more than 3,000 men. Washington dismissed that idea easily, arguing that it made sense only if the constitution could also require all foreign powers that wanted to attack the United States to limit *their* armies to no more than 3,000 men.

Gerald R. Ford

Franklin took the point, but wasn't about to drop his objections. Quite the contrary, he restated them more forcefully — and humorously — than ever, drawing upon an earthy metaphor to make his case clear. "A standing army," he drawled, "is like an erect member. While it provides excellent assurance for domestic tranquillity, it often invites temptation for foreign adventures."

In our century, Franklin Roosevelt maintained the tradition of Washington, Franklin, and Lincoln. Will Rogers once told the story of visiting the White House and being greeted by Eleanor Roosevelt.

"Where is the president?" Rogers asked.

"Wherever you hear the laughter," the First Lady replied.

As Liz Carpenter observes, that's the way the White House should be.

Roosevelt's White House was like Lincoln's in its reliance on humor as a way of lighting a path through dark times. Liz Carpenter recalls the story of Winston Churchill's visit there during the dark days of World War II. Relations between the two allied leaders were touchy, with each suspecting the other of concealing his true agenda. Finally, late one night after taking a shower, Churchill peeked out of the Lincoln bedroom, where he was staying, and saw that the light was still on in President Roosevelt's study. Slipping on a bathrobe, the British prime minister padded down the hall, stood in the doorway of the study, and opened the robe, revealing to FDR that he wasn't wearing any pajamas — or anything else — underneath.

"As you can see, Mr. President," Churchill rumbled, "I have nothing to hide."

It's not just presidents and prime ministers for whom humor makes life bearable. Lou Cannon, the veteran White House correspondent of the *Washington Post,* points out that humor sustains everyone connected with politics — candidates and reporters alike. "It is absolutely impossible," he says, "to go out on that campaign trail and be out there day after day, week after week, or to cover the White House and do all the things you have to do, without a sense of humor." His recollections of two decades covering national politics certainly reflect that.

Humor and the Presidency

To Lou's way of thinking, there is not a lot to be said about humor and the Nixon White House. As he puts it, the bottom line on Nixonian humor may have been summed up by a story related by a former colleague of Mr. Nixon's in the House of Representatives, a congressman from Long Beach, California. It seems that during Nixon's terms as vice president, a group of friends who had served with him in the House decided to throw a party for him. With that in mind, they called his secretary, Rosemary Woods, and said, "We would like some funny stories about Mr. Nixon." There was a pause at the other end of the line, and then Miss Woods replied: "There *are* no funny stories about Mr. Nixon."

That's not to say nothing humorous ever happened in the Nixon White House. People said funny things all the time, often without realizing it. Lou Cannon's favorite remark was one delivered by Ron Ziegler, Nixon's press secretary, during one of his annual reviews of the year's events for the press. Generally speaking, when a press secretary does one of these kinds of reviews, he tries to gloss over the bad moments and stress the good ones. Even so, as Lou recalls it, Ziegler outdid himself. "We had a good year," he told the assembled reporters, "except for Watergate." As far as Lou and most of the rest of the press were concerned, that was like saying the Titanic had a terrific maiden voyage, except for that iceberg.

Gerald R. Ford

One of Lou's favorite moments during my administration involved a press conference at which journalist Fred Barnes asked what Lou considers to have been one of the best questions ever asked at a presidential news conference. He may be right, though I must say I didn't appreciate Fred's question at the time.

This was during the 1976 primary campaign, in which my main opponent for the Republican presidential nomination was Ronald Reagan. One big issue in that campaign was the pardon of Richard Nixon. Though I felt I had done the right thing, I wasn't exactly eager to call attention to that particular decision. Evidently, my reticence didn't escape Fred. He got up at the press conference and said: "Mr. President, two or three times today you talked about your 'predecessor,' and once you referred to "Lyndon Johnson's successor.' Are you trying to avoid saying the name 'Richard M. Nixon'?"

My answer was simple and succinct. I said, "Yes."

When they're not trying to trip up politicians, political reporters seem to spend most of their time trying to trip up each other. Practical jokes have long been a stock in trade of the White House press corps. My former press secretary, Ron Nessen, was involved in more than a few of them — and occasionally managed to persuade me to lend a hand. His account of his time in the Ford administration makes me wonder how he ever got any serious work done. This is how he describes the lighter side of life in the White House:

I guess the funniest practical joke we ever pulled involved the *Newsweek* White House correspondent, Tom DeFrank. Tom is a graduate of Texas A&M, and you know what they say about Aggies. In any case, one night, when President Ford was campaigning in Ohio, some members of the White House staff, in connivance with some of Tom's colleagues in the press corps, snuck a live sheep into his hotel room.

President Ford wasn't involved in the joke, but he did hear about it. And when he saw Tom the next morning, the first thing he said was, "I hear you had a visitor in your room last night."

But Tom got his revenge, with yet another practical joke once again arranged with White House cooperation. This time the butt of the joke was one of the ringleaders of the sheep incident, Jim Naughton of the New York *Times*. What Tom did was to get Dick Cheney, the White House chief of staff, to tell Jim that if he showed up at Camp David the following Saturday at eight in the morning, the president would grant him an exclusive interview.

Naturally, Jim was excited. He'd had a request in for an interview with the president for quite some time. To make sure he wouldn't be late, he drove out to the Camp David area a day ahead of time and stayed overnight at some third-rate motel nearby. The next morning he turned up at the gates to Camp David promptly at eight. Needless to say, neither the guards nor anyone else at the presidential retreat had any instructions to admit him. President Ford wasn't even there that weekend. That was Tom DeFrank's revenge.

Humor and the Presidency

Jim Naughton was involved in another great practical joke, this one in San Diego, where President Ford was campaigning at one point. In between covering the president's appearances, Jim managed to find a place where he could buy the costume of the San Diego chicken, the mascot of the Padres baseball team. The next morning, the president held a news conference at the San Diego airport. As usual, the reporters had formed a kind of half-circle around him. Suddenly, out of the back of the crowd, the head of a giant chicken rose up.

The president didn't bat an eye. He simply finished the question he was answering, then said, "Yes, you, that chicken in the back, do you have a question?"

President Ford's own sense of humor was very subtle and wry and sophisticated. You may recall the trouble we got into during the 1976 campaign when, during one of the debates with Jimmy Carter, the president insisted that Poland was not under the domination of the Soviet Union. As a result of the uproar, President Ford was persuaded to make a public statement acknowledging that he had made a mistake and apologizing for it. Dick Cheney was working with him on the wording of the statement, and they went over it again and again to make sure it was properly done. Finally, when all the i's had been dotted and the t's had been crossed, Dick turned to the president and asked, "Now, do you know exactly what you're going to say?"

Absolutely deadpan, President Ford nodded and replied: "Yes, I'm going to go out there and

I'm going to tell the public that the Soviet Union does not dominate Poland."

Clearly, President Ford was not above poking fun at himself. Towards the end of his administration, after he had lost the election, he was talking to a group of reporters about what he might do after he left the White House. One possibility he said he was considering was becoming a professor at the University of Michigan. Then he paused, and added: "I'm not going to teach Eastern European history, however."

President Ford's humorous way of looking at things sometimes reaped substantive political results. For example, in the winter of 1975, just before Christmas, Congress was about to pass a $28 billion tax cut that the White House had proposed — and then go off on vacation without passing the related $28 billion budget cut that the administration had also asked for. Knowing the Hill, Ford got an idea. He instructed the White House congressional liason office to ask the parliamentarian of Congress what the rules were for calling Congress back to Washington for a special session during the Christmas recess. "Now, make sure that you tell the parliamentarian that I want to keep this an absolute secret," he told his aides. "That will get the word around the Hill faster than Western Union."

Sure enough, word got around, and Congress passed a compromise budget cut before adjourning.

David Kennerly, the president's personal photographer, probably had the most irreverent

125

sense of humor in the White House. Perhaps the best example was the night Saigon fell, a very sad time for all of us. David came into the National Security Council office, where President Ford was monitoring the situation, and announced: "Well, I have good news and bad news. The good news is the Vietnam War is over. The bad news is we lost."

My own sense of humor tended to run to gaffes and mistakes. The worst one I ever made was a time when I thought I was saying the right thing. (Actually, I always thought I was saying the right thing.)

This was just before the 1976 presidential primary in New Hampshire. President Ford was having a meeting in the White House one day with Lowell Thomas, the great old radio newscaster. Thomas also happened to be an avid skier, and while making small talk he asked the president if he was going to be skiing in New Hampshire that year. President Ford shook his head. "Naw," he said. "You know, when I was going to college I used to go up there to ski, but you could never tell what the conditions were going to be. And it was often very icy. So I'm not going to ski there now."

A day or two later, one of the Associated Press's White House correspondents casually asked me the same question — would the president be skiing in New Hampshire this year? Now, whenever I answered questions from the press, I always tried to imagine what President Ford would have said if he was there. This time I thought I was on really solid ground. After all, I had just heard the president answer this very

Gerald R. Ford

question just a few days earlier. So I said, "Naw, he's not going to ski in New Hampshire. It's too icy."

Of course, what I hadn't considered was the fact that skiing is probably the number one industry in the state. The reaction from New Hampshire to the president's apparent criticism of skiing conditions there was so angry that I began to worry that the president might lose the primary because of my stupid remark. One of the New Hampshire newspapers even ran an editorial about it, referring to me as "Reagan's little helper." I think the problem was that I had violated a cardinal rule for any public official — don't screw up on a slow news day.

Few high officials knew how to handle the press better than Henry Kissinger, who served both my predecessor and me as secretary of state. But even Henry had trouble getting the last word. Richard Growald, the veteran correspondent who covered the White House for UPI for a good part of my presidency, recalls the time Henry confronted him on the plane after a trip to Peking. As Growald tells the story, the secretary of state enjoyed telling the reporters who followed him around about the scrapbook his father kept. Supposedly, it contained a page devoted to each reporter who covered Henry, on which Papa Kissinger would paste every article that particular reporter had written about his son — until, that is, the reporter wrote something bad. When that happened, his father would rip the page out — and as Kissinger liked to put it, there went the reporter's chance for immortality.

On this particular occasion, Henry was steamed at Growald because of a story the UPI man had filed from Peking. As a result, Kissinger said, Growald's page was

127

being ripped out of his father's scrapbook. "What you did back in Peking," Henry fumed, "was unspeakable."

Baffled by Kissinger's ire, Growald asked what it was that he had done.

Henry's complaint was simple. "You wrote that when I arrived in Peking there were no flags and no bands playing at the airport," he said.

Kissinger was right. Growald *had* written that, and he admitted as much. The thing was, Growald added, it was true — when Kissinger had arrived in Peking, there weren't any bands playing at the airport, and there weren't any flags.

"But," Kissinger protested, "there never *are* any bands or flags at the airport."

As Growald noted, some people are difficult to please.

To be fair to Henry, he was a master at defusing a tense situation with a funny line. Growald witnessed two particularly good examples of this.

The first one occurred on the secretary's plane during one of his rounds of shuttle diplomacy in the mideast. According to Growald, they were on their way to Damascus when the chief of Kissinger's Secret Service detail — who happened to be a great favorite of Henry's — went back to the galley to get some food. One of the Uzi submachine guns the Secret Service uses was laying on top of a box of bread, and the agent picked it up to get to the bread. Just as he did, the plane dipped suddenly and the Uzi slipped from his grasp. Evidently, the safety was off, and when the gun hit the floor, it fired a round. Though no damage was done, the shocked agent was overcome with the realization that he could have killed someone. As a result, he did a perfectly natural thing — he fainted.

When he came to, Henry was standing over him. "Why didn't you tell me you wanted off the detail?" he asked the stricken agent. Before the agent could react,

Henry turned to the rest of his entourage. "Can you believe it?" he growled. "I'm the only man in the world who would have a bodyguard who would decide to shoot himself with a submachine gun at a distance of six inches. And miss."

The other story took place in Helsinki, during our historic summit meeting there. As Growald relates it, Ron Nessen and Bob Hartman, my chief speechwriter, were putting the word around, in strictest confidence, that Kissinger wouldn't be secretary of state for much longer. Good reporter that he is, Growald went immediately to Henry to get his comment. Characteristically, Kissinger was unfazed. "Who cares?" he shrugged. "After four years of Haldeman and Erlichman, I'm going to worry about Nessen and Hartman?"

Very few figures in government display the kind of deftness with the press that Kissinger routinely demonstrated. My successor, Jimmy Carter, certainly had more than his share of troubles with the press. But even he managed to get his own back. Liz Carpenter tells the story of one of his final appearances in Washington before leaving the White House. At a farewell dinner given him by the press corps, President Carter ended his speech to the group by saying, "I want to thank all of you who made my job so easy and enjoyable and comfortable." And then he turned to his wife and said, "Thank you, Rosalynn." As Liz notes, not a bad exit line.

Liz makes the point that a politician is usually best off employing the kind of humor that comes most naturally to him or her. "Ed Muskie, for example, was marvelous when he was telling spare stories about New England," she says. "And Lyndon Johnson was never good at telling Martha's Vineyard stories. Unfortunately, a lot of his speechwriters, whom he had inherited from John Kennedy, were always writing Martha's Vineyard jokes for him. He didn't even know where Martha's Vineyard was. He

129

thought it was some woman's winery. He was at his best when he told Johnson City stories."

President Johnson invariably used such stories to make a political point. One classic Johnson City tale he told was meant to indicate his feelings about the vast number of consultants and consulting firms that have proliferated in Washington over the years. The story concerns a bulldog in Johnson City that made all the female dogs in town pregnant every spring. Eventually the ladies of Johnson City got so fed up that they got together and had the bulldog fixed. Nonetheless, the next spring all the female dogs were pregnant again.

"It's that damned old bulldog again," said one of the ladies.

"But didn't we have him fixed?" asked another.

"We did," the first one replied. "But now he's acting as a consultant."

Johnson, of course, was an extremely demanding boss — so much so that it took a real sense of humor to work for him. As Liz tells it, he could be a compulsive workaholic who couldn't abide the notion of idle hands. She tells of the time, early in his presidency, when the Secret Service increased the size of the detail guarding the president at the LBJ Ranch in Texas. "There were about thirty agents down there," Liz recalls, "and one day the president walked into the kitchen and found them all standing around drinking coffee — *his* coffee. And that made him crazy. He wanted them to be doing something. So he turned around, just bristling, and he yelled at them: 'Swat flies!' They all stared at him for a moment. Then Rufus Youngblood, the chief of the White House detail, picked up a fly swatter and said: 'Well, I guess flies *are* a security problem.' "

The press, of course, isn't so easily dealt with. As Fred Barnes of *The New Republic* puts it, the motto of reporters in Washington is: "If you don't have anything nice to say, let's hear it." Here is Fred's account of the kind of political humor that only occasionally gets into print but fills the air at Washington cocktail parties:

Reporters love to make jokes about Ronald Reagan and his work habits. You know, those tough four-hour days. As Pat Paulsen observed, sometimes Reagan has to show up at the office twice a week. And the other day somebody said that Reagan was taking a working nap.

The way President Reagan deflects an over-eager aide who is pressing him to make a decision on something immediately is to say, "I want to sleep on it a while." With Reagan, the joke goes, you know he gets right to it.

Of course, Reagan is pretty good about this sort of thing. In a recent speech to the White House Correspondents Association, he joked about his work habits himself. He'd really been working hard, he told them, burning the midday oil.

And Reagan certainly knows how to get his own back. One of my favorite stories concerns his trip to China. While he was there he made a speech on Chinese television to the Chinese people. Evidently, the Chinese government didn't want some of what he had to say to be heard by the people, and some parts of the speech were blocked out. Afterwards, the American reporters travelling with the president rushed over to get his reaction. Was he going to stand for such censorship? How could he allow the Chinese to obscure the message he was trying to get out to the people?

Reagan's response was classic. He just smiled at the White House reporters and said,

"Oh, it didn't bother me at all. You guys do it to me all the time."

Presidents are hardly the only target of jokes. Presidential contenders draw a fair share — especially perennial candidates like Teddy Kennedy. The way you are supposed to tell whether Teddy is running or not is by his weight. If he is gaining weight, eating ice cream and so on, then he's not running. And so we know he's not running now, not just because he's said he isn't running, but because he's also a bit beefy.

How beefy is he? There is no end of jokes about Teddy's weight. A writer for the *Boston Globe* says you know where Kennedy stands, because there's a dent in the ground. He also claims that when Teddy goes to McDonald's, you can see the numbers on the sign out front going up. And that Teddy's campaign motto is, "If you can't take the heat in the kitchen, then eat the cookies in the living room." So much for the Senator from Pizza Hut, as he's getting to be known.

As the 1988 presidential race heats up, George Bush is becoming an increasingly popular target. Of course, he provides a lot of grist for the mill — like the time he went to the Middle East and asked a guide: "How dead is the Dead Sea?" The answer came back: "Very."

Bush's problem, of course, is what is called the wimp factor. As the joke goes, you know why Jeanne Kirkpatrick would be the perfect vice-presidential running mate for Bush? Because she'd add some macho to the ticket.

Then there's the accusation that Bob Dole made about Jack Kemp — that Kemp wanted a

tax break for hair spray. And Kemp's report —
that he was sorry to hear about the fire at the Dole
Library. Both books were destroyed.

It can get pretty vicious, as Treasury Secretary Jim Baker demonstrated at the 1985 Gridiron Club dinner. Baker told a story about a
dream he supposedly had in which President
Reagan, Republican Senate leader Bob Dole, and
longtime Speaker of the House Tip O'Neill all
died and went to heaven. They got to the pearly
gates together, and stood there a while before a
voice finally boomed out: "President Reagan, go
into the room on the right." Reagan did as he was
told, and found himself in a room with a mad dog.
"President Reagan," the voice explained, "you
have sinned, and must spend all eternity in this
room with this mad dog."

Meanwhile, Dole and O'Neill were still
outside. After a moment, the voice spoke again.
"Mr. Dole," it intoned, "go into the room directly
in front of you." Dole obediently followed the
instructions, and wound up in a room with a
gorilla. "Senator, you have sinned," the voice told
him, "and you must spend all of eternity in this
room with this gorilla."

By this time, Tip O'Neill was getting pretty
nervous. Finally, the voice spoke to him, telling
him to go into the room on the left. Understandably apprehensive, Tip did. To his delight and
relief, he found himself alone in a room with Bo
Derek. And the voice boomed out: "Bo Derek, you
have sinned. . . ."

**Humor and the
Presidency**

Six

More
Stories

****

Few men are as expert in — and funny about — the practice of politics as Lyn Nofziger. Originally a reporter, Lyn has earned a reputation over the years as one of the shrewdest political gurus around, and he has served as political adviser to Presidents Nixon and Reagan. His views on humor and the presidency are worth repeating:

> Every once in a while I lay awake at night trying to think of two things: one is something funny that Richard Nixon said; the other is something funny that Jimmy Carter said. Invariably, I fail in both cases.
>
> But at least Dick Nixon could laugh. He could appreciate a joke or a quick retort. I remember once having a conversation with him just before I left the White House staff to go to work for the Republican National Committee. "Now, Nofziger," he said to me, "when you go to the National Committee, don't let them get away with a single lie."
>
> "Mr. President," I replied, "I'm not even going to let them get away with the truth."
>
> Nixon laughed, and then we went on to other things. A week or two later, to my surprise, I read my little quip in the *New York Times*. Not having planted it there myself, I asked someone

how it had gotten in the paper. "Well, the president was amused," the answer came back, "and he went around telling it to everybody."

The point of this is that people who think Nixon doesn't have a sense of humor are wrong. He just has a hard time expressing it.

Of course, many of the funniest things Nixon said were said by accident. I recall talking to him a couple of weeks after President Reagan was shot. "Now, Lyn," he said, "don't let the president make any decisions until he's completely well, because you don't make good decisions when you're sick." And then he added: "You know, I made the decision not to burn the tapes when I was recovering from pneumonia."

Speaking about Reagan, one of the things that impressed everybody about the way he handled the assassination attempt was his ability to make quips at the hospital, telling the doctors as he was wheeled into the operating room: "I hope all of you are Republicans."

Of course, President Reagan didn't realize he'd been shot until he got to the hospital. He thought he had broken a rib when the Secret Service threw him into the back of the presidential limousine and leaped on top of him. When they finally sat him up and he began to cough a little blood, he thought to himself: "Well, darn it, they've not only broken my ribs, they've punctured my lung."

In any case, once the extent of his injuries was known, he responded with those funny remarks. I've always thought that humor is a great catharsis. Certainly, President Reagan's ability to be funny at a time like that — his ability to show

Gerald R. Ford

138

that he could laugh and joke about what had happened — not only helped the staff and Nancy, it also helped the nation.

Ironically, the nation almost didn't find out about his funny remarks. Although I had once been Reagan's press secretary, I was not a part of the White House press operation at the time of the shooting. But because Jim Brady, who was the president's press secretary, had also been shot, they asked me to handle the press at the hospital. So I set up a press room in an auditorium nearby, and eventually we called a briefing. Needless to say, there were a lot of reporters there, and as usual they asked every stupid question in the world. They also asked a few intelligent ones, though the stupid outnumbered the intelligent by about ten to one. Finally, when we were all finished, I cut off the briefing. Then, just as I was walking out, somebody in the audience called out: "Did Reagan have anything to say?" And I thought, "Oh, my God!" I had totally forgotten to tell the press about Reagan's quips, which I had very carefully written down on a notecard that I had stashed in my pocket. So I pulled the quips out and read them to everyone. That, of course, turned out to be one of the most important parts of the story, for it was the quips that reassured the nation that the president was all right. Yet, as I say, I came within an ace of forgetting all about them. If that reporter hadn't yelled out that question, they might still be in my pocket today.

Reagan, of course, is a very interesting man when it comes to humor. He loves to use it in his speeches. Some of it is relevant to what he has to say, some of it is just to lighten the mood. But

Humor and the Presidency

139

people who think that Reagan makes up his own jokes are wrong. He'll steal humor where he can find it. And then he'll turn it to his own ends.

As an individual, what's interesting about Reagan is that he's managed to keep a sense of humor about himself. Watching him go from actor to governor to president, you can worry: "Well, can I still kid him? Has he gotten so darned important that you can't treat him like a normal human being?" The answer is that you can. Like President Ford, President Reagan has managed to keep his sense of humor, which I think has done a lot to maintain his sense of perspective.

I recall a time that President Reagan and I and a speechwriter of his were going up in the elevator from the ground floor of the White House to the living quarters. The president looked at me and said, "Gee, Lyn, I remember you when you were young." Without thinking, I replied, "Gee, Mr. President, I don't remember you when you were young." The speechwriter, who didn't know the president very well, cringed. But Reagan just laughed, and we went about our business. It's pure coincidence that I left the White House shortly thereafter.

Not only does President Reagan have a good sense of humor, he's also one of the great joke-tellers of all time. He's particularly good on dialect jokes. In fact, I think one of the major mistakes the president made was listening to the critics who ganged up on him after he told a particular joke in New Hampshire during the 1980 campaign. I've forgotten all the details, but it involved an Italian gentleman, a Polish gentleman, and a fight between a duck and a rooster. As

Gerald R. Ford

140

I recall, the Italian was the one who made sure that the duck would win, and the Pole was the one who bet on the duck. In any case, it was a very funny joke. But somebody in the press heard it and wrote a story about how terrible it was that Ronald Reagan was going around telling Polish jokes. Unfortunately, instead of simply saying, "Look, that happens to be a funny joke, and I will tell it again," the president listened to some terrible advice and said, "Well, I was just telling this joke as an illustration of the kind of joke you shouldn't tell."

The fact is, Ronald Reagan likes jokes. He likes hearing them and he likes telling them. He's the kind of man who likes to leave a meeting in a good humor, and almost invariably he has a joke to tell somewhere towards the end of every meeting. That's nice, because then people go away feeling good, forgetting the fact that he may have stuck it to them in the middle of the meeting.

At bottom, I think that presidential humor can serve many purposes. It cannot only help you win re-election — which I guess is the most important thing — but it can help the people you're dealing with. It can help the country by setting a mood. I think we are fortunate when we have presidents who have a sense of humor, presidents who can sit back and look at things and relax, instead of worrying who's playing tennis on the White House courts. Because when the president is relaxed, I think the whole country is relaxed.

Another keen political wit with a unique insight on humor and the presidency is former congressman Donald Rumsfeld, who served in my administration as both secre-

141

tary of defense and White House chief of staff. His comments on the subject are equally interesting:

Gerald R. Ford

There are all kinds of humor that a president can use. Jack Kennedy, of course, was a great wit. As president, he used what you might call deflecting humor. For example, I recall there was a big to-do over the fact that Stewart Udall, his interior secretary, had been extracting campaign contributions from all the major corporations that were beholden to the interior department. As a result, the press was just all over him. Things reached fever pitch the night of a major black-tie fundraising dinner. But Kennedy was wonderful. He got up and thanked the guests for their wonderful generosity, he thanked the chairmen of all the committees for their hard work, and he thanked Stewart Udall for handling the publicity.

At that moment, the problem was gone. It was *over*.

There's also gallows humor. I remember how upset Senator Bob Mathias was at the 1964 Republican convention. Mathias, of course, was a liberal Republican, and he was bordering on the apoplectic over the party's nomination of Barry Goldwater. This particular night he was standing in the back of the hall, while down front Dwight Eisenhower was giving a speech. And I heard Mathias mumble to himself, as he thought about Goldwater becoming the Republican candidate, "This would never have happened if Eisenhower was still alive."

Businessmen who come to Washington bring what you might call industrial humor. I recently took part in a panel discussion with a number of other former White House chiefs of staff at which General Andrew Goodpaster, who worked for President Eisenhower, provided an excellent example of industrial humor. During the Eisenhower administration a super-efficient Pentagon briefer addressed a special meeting of the National Security Council. He had flip charts and he had visual aids. He was supposed to be on for twelve minutes, and he was on for twelve minutes. He had a three-part presentation, each part of which had three parts. He took three questions, and then he walked out.

When the guy was gone, Charlie Wilson, the former head of General Motors who was Eisenhower's secretary of defense, turned to Goodpaster and said: "You know, that fella's got too much horsepower for his flywheel."

That's industrial humor.

Humor can also be used to divert a president. At the same panel discussion I just mentioned, John Chancellor, the NBC commentator, who was serving as moderator, posed a wonderful question to the assembled chiefs of staff: "What could you do as White House chief of staff," he asked, "when your president was about to do something *really* stupid. After all, no one is perfect. Everyone makes mistakes. At some point your president must have gotten up a head of steam for whatever reason to do something really dumb. Now, it's your job to grab hold of him. How would you handle that?"

Everyone was kind of quiet for a moment. Then Ted Sorensen, who worked for President Kennedy, spoke up. "We didn't do too well in the

143

first six months," he said. "You'll recall the Bay of Pigs and a few other things. But we finally developed a formula that worked. What we did was to let President Kennedy get a good head of steam up, and then we'd sidle up to him and say: 'You know, Mr. President, that's a terrific idea. That's exactly the way Dick Nixon would handle it.'"

We all laughed, except for Bob Haldeman. "But I couldn't use *that*," he complained.

Gerald R. Ford

Then there's unintentional humor. I remember one day when I was in the White House as an assistant to Richard Nixon. I was minding my own business, when the President and George Shultz called me in and said, "We want you to run the wage and price controls for the United States of America."

"But I don't believe in wage and price controls," I said.

"We know," they replied. "That's why we want you to run them."

I remember another example from that period. We were having problems controlling the price of food. So Herb Stein, the chairman of the Council of Economic Advisers, held a press conference at which he explained that inflation was the result of too many dollars chasing too few goods and services. And then he concluded by pointing out that "what we've really discovered during this first peacetime experiment with wage-price controls in the history of the United States of America is that one of the last things that the American people are willing to give up is food."

That did not go over well — which brings me to the Ford administration. I was with President Ford in the car racing to the airport one day after he had completed a political speech in Hartford, Connecticut. As is the usual practice, the Hartford police had blocked off all the streets. Nevertheless, some young kids managed to crash their hot rod into the side of the presidential limousine. No one was hurt, but we were all thrown to the floor.

Now this was an unusual experience. In fact, it was the only time in history that a presidential limousine has ever been hit by another car. Still, the Secret Service knew exactly how to react. They have a strict policy to handle such situations, which is to assume it's a conspiracy, that there are other people involved, and that the thing to do is *get the president out of there!* So the lead car took off, and the presidential limousine took off, and the tail car took off. Then the lead car stopped, whereupon the presidential limousine bashed into the back of the lead car, and the tail car bashed into the back of the limousine. It was very much like a Marx Brothers movie.

A few years later — to be exact, the day after the 241 American Marines were killed in Beirut — President Reagan asked me to become his Middle East envoy and spend some time over there. So I travelled around the Middle East, and at one point found myself in Beirut, which happens to be a war zone. While I was there, staying at the ambassador's residence, the fighting escalated, and we were trapped for four or five days. There were Russian-made rockets landing all over the yard, and snipers shooting at the place. Most of the windows and skylights had been blown out, and we were sleeping in flak jackets. It was not the best place to be. The main comfort I

Humor and the Presidency

had was the knowledge that the ambassador and the president's Middle East envoy were being protected by the most elite security team America could provide.

There were only about three or four of us in the place, which was falling apart all around us. There was no basement, no place to go. We just sat there in our flak jackets. One afternoon, I was sitting under a staircase having a cup of coffee with the head of the elite security team, and I asked him where he was from.

"Hartford," he replied.

"Well," I said, "what did you do there?"

"I was a policeman."

As that great American philosopher, Satchel Paige, used to day: "Never look back. They may be gaining on you."

The point is, the funniest incidents are often funny only in retrospect.

There's another incident with President Ford that comes to mind. We were out in San Francisco, where the president was giving a talk to the construction trades. As I recall, four or five of us left the hall with the president after the speech, and we got onto a freight elevator, the kind whose doors open and close from the top rather than the sides. Now, this was a period when the president had bumped his head four or five times on national television, and the last thing we wanted was more of that kind of publicity. Needless to say, as we were getting on the elevator, the door fell. And since President Ford was the tallest one in the group, it was his head that the door fell on.

It was awful. He wasn't hurt, but there was

an ugly, two-inch red welt that ran right across his bald forehead like a neon sign. We managed to get him into the limousine and back up to our suite at the St. Francis hotel without anyone seeing him, but then we were stuck. The president was supposed to depart from the hotel and wave to the crowd and then make a campaign appearance. How in the world was he going to do that without the press seeing that he had hit his head again?

Someone suggested that we get him a hat. Someone else suggested a wig. A third aide was looking for a cosmetic bag so we could put some powder on him to cover it up. Well, I was chief of staff, and chiefs of staff sometimes have to take charge. So I decided that we would just brazen it out. We went downstairs, and the president walked through the crowd waving at people, and then — as you may remember — a crazy woman tried to shoot him.

Immediately, we shoved the president into the limousine and raced out of there. I was on top of the president, and the head of the Secret Service detail was on top of me. After about six blocks, President Ford said, "Hey, Rummy, you guys are heavy. Get off!"

Pretty soon, we arrived at Air Force One, and to this day no one ever knew that the president had bumped his head again.

As Don Rumsfeld points out, humor is often a useful tool to cool down an angry president. Harry Middleton, who served as a speechwriter for Lyndon Johnson, tells of the time he travelled with LBJ to Detroit, where the president was going to make a major speech on the Vietnam War to a veterans group. Enroute, Middleton was summoned into the president's cabin on Air Force One. LBJ, it seemed, wasn't happy with the speech Middleton had written for him. "We've got to be tougher than this speech says," he insisted. "I want you to put in here that the people who are bad-mouthing our policy have to stand up and be counted, and go over there and take their places beside our boys in the trenches in Vietnam."

To Middleton, that made no sense. For one thing, he thought, there were no trenches in Vietnam. For another, he couldn't see the logic of asking dissenters to go over and fight a war that they opposed. So he went back to his cabin scratching his head. A few minutes later, LBJ's press secretary, George Christian, came out of the president's cabin and said to Middleton: "You can't put that in the speech, you know. The press would eat us alive."

Still, something had to be done. So the two of them worked out some new language, a bit tougher than what Middleton had originally written but not quite what LBJ had asked for. They had the new version typed up, and a few hours later they stood in the back of the hall in Detroit while President Johnson delivered the speech, wondering if he would read it as written, or as he sometimes did, extemporize.

As it turned out, the president delivered the speech just as Middleton and Christian had written it. But back on board Air Force One, on the return trip to Washington, LBJ once again summoned Middleton into his cabin. This time General William Westmoreland, the Army chief of staff and former Vietnam commander, was with the president. Westmoreland had been at the veterans meeting, and Johnson had invited him to return to Washington aboard the presidential plane.

At first, LBJ was quite friendly, offering Middleton a seat and asking the steward to bring him a drink. But then

148

he got down to business. "I didn't see in that speech you gave me the things I wanted you to put in it," Johnson growled at him.

"No, sir," Middleton replied.

The president frowned. "Would you mind telling me why?"

"Well, Mr. President," Middleton said, "I thought that on reflection you probably would really not want to say it just the way you put it to me."

"Oh, you did, did you? You thought I didn't mean what I said." Johnson turned to Westmoreland. "General, did you hear that?"

Westmoreland nodded, whereupon LBJ proceeded to tell him exactly what he had wanted Middleton to put into the speech — how the people who were badmouthing his Vietnam policy ought to stand up and be counted and take their place beside our boys in the trenches. "Now, General," the president concluded, "what would you do if one of your officers decided that you didn't really mean an order that you had given? How would you handle that?"

Middleton stood there silently as Westmoreland considered his answer. "Well, Mr. President," the general finally replied, "I think these things have to be decided on a case by case basis."

Johnson nodded.

"In this case," Westmoreland went on, "I think Harry did us all a favor, because I don't know what we would have done with those sons of bitches over there."

The president laughed, and Middleton was off the hook.

Such incidents aside, one of the nice things about being president is that your staff generally has to do what you tell them — no matter how difficult it may be. In such cases, a sense of humor is often essential. Dick Cheney, who had more than his share of difficult assignments when he

149

worked for me in the White House, recalls two classic examples:

Gerald R. Ford

> All of us who served in the Ford administration will always remember all those hard-fought primary contests in the spring of 1976, as we battled our way from New Hampshire in February to the convention in Kansas City that August. After a 1,300-vote victory for Ford in New Hampshire, and then slightly bigger victories in Florida and Illinois, and then a Reagan victory in North Carolina, the race turned into a real see-saw contest, eventually getting down to the point where every single delegate counted.
>
> As a result, the White House launched a massive effort to try to sway every single uncommitted delegate we could get our hands on. There wasn't anything we wouldn't do for an uncommitted delegate. We would fly them in by the planeload from around the country, bringing them to Washington for briefings and to the White House for cocktails with the president.
>
> There were always problems with switchers. We had one Republican delegate from Brooklyn who used to change sides each week. Granted, anybody from Brooklyn who is a Republican is a little strange anyway. But we brought her down to the White House repeatedly, and the president finally closed the deal when we brought in about forty of her relatives. He took them into the Oval Office and met with them for about two hours — all for one vote. That was how hard we worked for those delegates.
>
> The ultimate goodie was the Bicentennial

visit of Queen Elizabeth of England. The formal white tie and tail dinner marking the occasion at the White House was, of course, the high point of the social season that year, and a lot of distinguished Americans were invited in to dine with Her Majesty. It just happened that a number of those distinguished Americans were also uncommitted delegates.

In the midst of all this turmoil in the summer of 1976, we had a crisis develop at the White House. Late one night, while the First Family was upstairs in the private quarters, a man jumped the fence outside the White House and went charging towards the mansion carrying a long piece of pipe. The police officer who was on duty did exactly what he should have done. He hollered at the man to stop. The intruder ignored him, and kept going. So the officer pulled out his pistol and fired a warning shot. But the man still kept going. Finally, the officer did the only thing he could — he took careful aim and shot the intruder, dropping him dead on the spot.

At that point, all hell broke loose. Sirens were going off, ambulances and police cars were racing up. It was chaos. The young officer, who had been on the force only a short time, was understandably shaken up by the experience. In an effort to settle him down, we brought him into the Secret Service control post under the West Wing of the White House. As he sat there, trying to calm down, one of his colleagues walked up, put his hand on the officer's shoulder, and said, "You know, we're gonna be in an awful lot of trouble with the president if that fella you shot was an uncommitted delegate."

Humor and the Presidency

That should give you some idea of the intensity of the contest.

In the end, of course, we won the nomination. And at the 1976 Republican convention in Kansas City, after Bob Dole was selected as President Ford's running mate, we had a hurry-up meeting at which the president and Senator Dole decided that it would be nice after the convention ended to fly straight to Dole's hometown of Russell, Kansas, and hold a rally. They thought this was a great idea. Unfortunately, as the staff man who had worked for weeks putting together the national convention, I knew that our advance crew was completely exhausted. Everyone had been up all night for weeks. What we were all looking forward to was flying to Vail, Colorado, where we could take a short break before starting to plan the fall campaign.

But the president was bound and determined that we would stop first in Russell, Kansas. As I recall, we had a rather heated argument about it. My point was that, as this would be the first stop after the nomination, it had to be a major campaign event. "We can't afford to have anything less than a first-class event," I told him. "Unless we can pull one off, we really shouldn't go."

President Ford, who by now was a little red in the cheeks, ended the debate by poking me in the chest and saying, "By God, we're going to Russell, Kansas."

So we did.

Now, President Ford had no idea how much work went into putting together a first-class presidential event. To begin with, Russell, Kansas, does not have an airport, which means you can't fly into it. That meant putting people on Greyhound buses. We also had to buy radio time all over the western half of the state to tell people where and when the rally would be. After all, it doesn't do any good to take a president someplace if people don't know he's going to be there.

It took tremendous effort. Once again, the advance crew worked all night getting the word out, getting things set up, making all the preparations. Finally, we flew the president in Air Force One to the nearest airport, which was fifty miles away, and helicoptered him from there to Russell. We landed in a corn field right next to the town. As a result of our efforts, the place was packed. There were bodies everywhere. It looked like half of Kansas had turned out.

Surveying the scene, the president leaned over and tapped me on the knee. "You see," he said. "I knew we'd get a crowd."

Seven

Only Human
* * * * * * *

One of the most bizarre events I remember from my presidency was when the newly installed White House swimming pool was finally completed and I was going to take my first swim. Word got out, and, for reasons I have never understood, the White House press corps made that swim one of the biggest, best-covered "non-events" of my administration.

Dave Kennerly and Bob Barrett, who was then my military aide, were with me on the Sunday afternoon of the infamous swim. When Barrett hesitantly informed me that photographers were present to cover the occasion, I should have known by his behavior that something was going on.

Anyway, I asked him who was covering it. "Everybody," he said.

Sure enough, I went outside and there, lined up alongside of the pool, were more than two dozen photographers waiting to catch this truly historical swim by "the leader of the Free World."

I would have loved to have walked out to the pool carrying an inflated rubber duck or somesuch. In fact, we made an effort to dig one up, but we couldn't find one in time.

In any event, the photographers snapped me diving into the pool and climbing out of the pool, doing the sidestroke, the breaststroke, and the Australian crawl. It was quite a spectacle. It was also silly, and I knew it. So did the photographers who'd been assigned to take my picture.

Humor and the Presidency

157

Still, there was a good reason to go along with it. As in so many other instances, in allowing the coverage, we created a bond between the people in front of and the people behind the cameras. Somewhere down the line, you figure, those photographers will have the option of whether or not to take a less than flattering picture of you. Or maybe they'll be choosing one picture over another to send to their editor. When those options present themselves, I would like to believe (though I can't prove it) that if they don't regard you as a pretentious president in a pretentious White House, they might choose to give you a break. At a critical moment, such consideration can have significant effects.

Gerald R.
Ford

★ ★ ★

Humor is very important to the nation. People are trying to make sense out of what they read in the newspapers or watch on television. The complexity of an economic policy, a trade agreement, or an arms reduction pact can be baffling even to those working on such projects on a full-time basis. John and Jane Q. Public have problems and responsibilities of their own. He or she is probably going to work each day, maybe putting kids through college or worrying about getting a new car or who knows what. Given all this, people who want to develop an opinion on some national or international policy need some shortcuts, some easy way to get to the heart of a complicated but important question. Humor can come in very handy in this context. People can identify with a leader who has a sense of humor.

Moreover, these days the stock market, gold prices, and the value of the dollar can all be dramatically affected by the words or behavior of a president. Without humor to break up the seemingly endless continuum of crises and problems, we'd be in a terrible fix.

During the primary campaign of 1976, when Ron Reagan and I were going at it toe to toe, the Panama Canal became a very hot issue. One Saturday evening I was scheduled to give a speech, and it was inevitable that the audience expected some comment from me on the issue. Ron and his people had done an excellent job of getting the subject to the boiling point — so much so that to make a comment about the Panama Canal would only fan the flames, and we didn't want to fall into that trap.

How do you deal with something like that? We turned to humor. When I came out to give my speech, I was wearing a Panama hat. We had sent Barrett out that afternoon to find one. The audience loved it, and I proceeded to speak about everything but the Panama Canal.

That was helpful humor. It allowed the people in the audience to know more about my feeling than words would have ever conveyed. It also put the issue in perspective. The unspoken message was, "Hey, remember, this is the political season. Let's not take this public display of differences between Americans too seriously."

Politicians, especially presidents, want to be liked. That may sound trite, but making yourself liked is far more easily said than done. And it is a distinctly unpleasant experience to be told that, according to the results of a poll, your popularity is at an all-time low. You can say to yourself, "I'm just a hard working guy from Grand Rapids doing the best I can. Why don't people like me?" Well, let me tell you — if you lament over that question for more than five seconds, you might as well walk away from the job. For the president, there are no sure things, no safe harbors, and no uncontroversial issues. As Harry Truman said, "If you can't stand the heat, get out of the kitchen!"

That brings me to another point. Humor, like beauty,

Humor and the Presidency

159

can be in the eyes of the beholder. It would be wrong to give the impression that I enjoyed or understood all the humorous incidents in which I found myself involved. Unfortunately, the line between humor and ridicule is thin indeed. True, the heat of political campaigns, for better or worse, toughens the skin of any politician. But make no mistake about it — many things still hurt. Just because a president doesn't publicly acknowledge a cartoon or derisive remark does not mean that the cartoonist or critic missed his mark. The fact is, any person in public life who says such slings and arrows do not hurt is a liar.

Gerald R.
Ford

All presidents, whether they like it or not, deal most often with humor that has them as the target. However, as in a football game, even a president can be on the offense some of the time.

The reference to football reminds me of Lyndon Johnson's suggestion that I played football too long without a helmet. To be sure, the first expression of that kind remark was certainly disparaging. However, over a period of time, some of my speechwriters and I were able to turn it around and have it become a useful ice-breaker in certain situations.

It's interesting to observe how the gentlemen sitting in the White House react to humor or use humor themselves. It might be said that a certain president didn't have a sense of humor. Though that might be true, it's more likely that the sense of humor existed but the individual did not allow it to be expressed in any public way.

Harry Truman, with his quick and crusty manner, certainly seemed to enjoy the give and take of pointed humor. Dwight Eisenhower, by contrast, maintained a more reserved, if not conservative, posture when it came to engaging in any repartee. His military background was probably responsible for his reserved public personality.

Democrats and Republicans alike envied John Kennedy's ability to keep potentially tense or confrontational situations light. The benefit of humor as practiced by Kennedy was obvious. Reporters love any comments that provide good copy. Just one well-turned phrase can give an enterprising reporter covering the White House something to write about on an otherwise slow news day.

Even though press conferences are always filled with peril, President Kennedy seemed to enjoy his time with the press. That's most important. As I mentioned earlier, avoiding an adversarial relationship with the media is not always easy, but it pays rich dividends. Despite all the criticism that has been heaped on many in the media, the fact is that journalists, both print and electronic, can be quite astute about intuitively determining what's true. It's when they become suspicious that the game of investigation and harassment begins. Humor, both extended and received, definitely helps the press stay in touch with the human being who occupies the Oval Office.

Presidents Nixon and Carter seemed less able or willing to establish a casual and confident rapport with the White House press corps. When difficult times developed during their administrations, the absence of a friendly relationship with the press created additional problems. Frankly, it doesn't take very much or very long for a president to get himself into a "no-win" situation. If reporters don't feel any kinship with the president or his staff, they will turn on him at the first opportunity.

President Reagan, with his remarkable communicative skills, has been superb in his use of humor with the public. I don't think the success he has had with the general public has necessarily extended to the media. Nonetheless, the press corps has definitely respected his ability to maintain his popularity. Mainly as a result of that popularity, the press treated Reagan extremely gently until the Iran arms controversy developed.

Humor and the Presidency

The truth of the matter is that the press and the president are competing for the same audience. That audience is the general public. For an extended period of time, President Reagan had the support of that audience — in large part because of his ability to use lighthearted and well-timed remarks.

★ ★ ★

Gerald R.
Ford

Humor doesn't only matter to me. I believe it matters to many, many Americans. There are times when you might as well laugh at yourself because you can be sure others are going to laugh at you. Unlike freedom of speech or freedom of the press, laughter is not specifically protected by an amendment to our Constitution. Nevertheless, it is probably the clearest and most resounding expression of freedom we have.

We are all human. We come from Michigan and California, New York, Florida, and Alabama. We work. We raise families. We love. And, thank God, we laugh.

The words of Ella Wheeler Wilcox really say it all:

> *Laugh and the world laughs with you,*
> *Weep and you weep alone;*
> *For the old earth must borrow its mirth,*
> *But has trouble enough of its own.*